Building a Thriving Therapy Business - The Secrets to My Success

HOW TO BE YOURSELF TO ATTRACT CLIENTS INTO YOUR LIFE

Clare Cogan

DEDICATION

This book in its entirety is dedicated to the memory of my beautiful, wonderful, courageous friend, Nicky Tarn, who lost her 6 year battle with cancer in 2015.

I miss her more than words can say but she left behind her legacy of tenacity, humour and tremendous courage in the face of adversity.

She opened my mind to endless possibilities, and the turmoil of grief and bereavement has been my drive to show others how we can make so much of the lives we have right now, and live them to the fullest.

ACKNOWLEDGMENTS

I cannot write this book without acknowledging my wonderful family who I love to the ends of the earth. My husband William, my sons, Joseph and Daniel, and our pup, Teddy. Without them I would not be the therapist I am today with the business I love.

William has supported me at every turn, even when he didn't understand the journey, he trusted my decision-making and I am forever grateful for that. My boys have given me the opportunity to grow and learn on my parenting journey, whilst building my therapy practice, and they embrace my 'alternative' approach with love and good humour. They are truly my raison d'etre.

HOW TO BE YOURSELF TO ATTRACT CLIENTS INTO YOUR LIFE

It's a story of many parts, and has no beginning, middle or end. This is not a self-help kinda book, more a book depicting my journey in the world of therapy, my successes, my pitfalls. Every day I see newly qualified therapists released out into the world with their certificates in their hands, feeling rightfully proud, with that fire burning in their belly. That's just how I was, back in 2007, full of excitement, anticipation, and plans.

I made the decision to train as a reflexologist when my oldest son was 10 months old. It wasn't that I woke up one day and decided I was going to 'become' a reflexologist. As with everything on my therapy journey, it just happened. I found the course, the timings worked, and I just got stuck in.

I had enjoyed positive reflexology experiences in the past, lovely treatments from a local reflexologist when I lived at home, but nothing really profound other than calming and relaxing experiences. I was an anxious teen, and a stressed out 20 something so I really did believe that alternative therapies calmed the body, and mind.

However, I was a bit of a blank canvas where reflexology was concerned, and I didn't really know what to expect.

The 10 months of my training were in fact the most demanding and exhausting of my time to date. Not only was I mum to a one-year-old who, throughout my course was moving into the joys of toddlerhood, I also was working part-time as a social worker for a local Fostering and Adoption Team.

Being a working mum evoked a lot of guilt for me – I loved my time as 'me', where I could do my job but then I equally loved immersing myself as mum for the other two-and-a-half days of my week.

Fitting in my numerous reflexology case studies took some doing, however, and the reality was that I had to work every evening just to keep up with the workload. My lack of time was actually a blessing in disguise because it kept me focused. I made sure every single treatment was written up as soon as I did it. That was how I coped and kept on top of the work.

So that was the practical, and academic side of the course sorted. To be honest I was always pretty good at doing what was expected of me - I'd learnt that skill from a young age - so in terms of 'achieving' I knew I would make the grade come hell or high water.

What I wasn't prepared for was the journey I would be taken on once I embraced the whole learning and understanding behind alternative health. I had gained two dress sizes during and after my pregnancy. This was, by my own admission, due to my poor eating habits.

When I was sat breastfeeding my son, my body was would crave fuel just to function. However, I was misled by my own understanding that I could eat whatever I liked, and because I was breastfeeding the extra weight would just shrink from my hips, just like that! Unfortunately, that was not the case, and as I grew in size my clothes shrunk, and it wasn't until midway through my course and a talk from a naturopath that I realised I needed to do something about my eating.

That was the first conscious change I made. Not big, not demonstrative, but just becoming more mindful about what I put in my body. Over the latter part of the course I began to notice the weight shifting, I felt better too and had more energy. I started to realise that my reflexology training really was a gift that had opened up my world to so many other streams of knowledge and understanding.

I carried on with my training, which truly did take over my spare time, and sapped any energy I had left after taking care of a lively toddler all day. We were also trying for a second baby towards the end of the course, too. Looking back now I am totally conscious of why it didn't happen. Life was far too full on!

I will never forget my final exam which came after all my case studies had been submitted (I told you I always kept on top of the game).

My son (via his dad) gave me a little troll to sit on my desk and a card which read, "If you don't know the answer, Mum, just point to the window and then everyone claps anyway".

There was a running joke in our house when we sang *Wind the Bobbin Up*, that whenever Joseph did the actions with us, everyone got really excited and happy. That made the exam so much easier to bear.

The summer was tough going, waiting for the results. I had grand plans. I was going to leave my part-time job, work exactly the hours I wanted to and build a thriving business.

We were given a bit of business training towards the end of our course, the advice and guidance bits and pieces we needed - such as the benefits of having a free phone number versus putting a mobile number on your cards, and the importance of having a website as well as a leaflet. It was basic, but informative, and set us on the right path, sort of.

I found out I had qualified the week I discovered I was pregnant with my second son (I didn't know he was a boy back then). We had fallen pregnant during a much-needed holiday for the three of us, time which I did use to work on writing my website using a hosting company who supplied the templates and helped with the dreaded SEO.

It looked pretty, it gave people all the info needed and once I returned from my holiday (and unfortunately started throwing up with the dreaded pregnancy sickness) I sat back and waited for the phone to start ringing to fill my diary with appointments.

And the phone stayed strangely silent. And my diary remained empty of reflexology clients.

I decided during my training that I was not going to hire out clinic rooms as I did not like to have specific appointment times and liked being able to treat at home. It was flexible, and that's always a bonus when you have children. The downside, however, was that I could only offer appointments, whenever I had childcare, which was often just at weekends.

Herein lies the first lesson – boundaries are the single most important thing a therapist can ever learn when setting up their business.

So, I sat there, waiting for the phone to ring, not really understanding why it wasn't, and I realised quite quickly that my dream of leaving my part-time job and growing the reflexology business was not going to sustain my income, just yet. As it was, I was dealing with a pretty turbulent pregnancy, and a lively toddler, and the end of a house extension - so I had my hands full anyway!

But, the beauty of learning and qualifying in a therapy like this means you never lose the actual skill of doing it, so time wasn't so crucial. But you do have to work on building your confidence.

The first non-friend-related booking came via a phone call and, safe to say, I was petrified. I knew my stuff, had done 100s of practice hours on a variety of different people, but I just couldn't stop feeling scared.

I now know that is normal, and expected, when we train to do something and put it out there for the first time. It's also why a lot of reflexologists don't make it over the first hurdle, because it can be a scary place.

After all, how can I go from training for free to charging reasonably for my time?

In truth, it was petrifying.

I did it though and for the next couple of years my clients were ad-hoc and varied, reaching me in various ways. But at that point in time, mainly through a Google search. I had accidently done well with my choice of domain name when I set up my website 'Marlow Reflexology'. The search engines loved it, so that helped me masses with being found locally.

So, now I had a young family, a part-time job and a therapy business. I was restricted to treating during the evening and weekends, and this did limit the number of clients I could see and treat. It also required my commitment to spend a day working in the office, or with the boys, and then focus on a client's needs. But I did it because I loved it, and reflexology still fascinated me.

The turning point in my business came when I moved away from the silent phone and physically got myself out there into the Marlow community.

My son started primary school and I decided to go to the school's Parent and Teacher meeting to familiarise myself with how I could help. During the meeting they were talking about organising an indulgence evening and asked whether anyone knew of any reflexologists!

Tentatively, I raised my hand, and there it was, me physically taking myself out from behind my comfy treatment room and website and out into the larger community, offering 10-minute taster treatments.

I absolutely loved it, and it raised enough awareness for a small trickle of enquiries and clients.

A few times I had to be brave, I had to follow up people who had expressed an interest in a treatment or learning more about reflexology but hadn't booked. So, I would phone them, or ask them face-to-face, quivering inside that they would say no or feel like I was being 'pushy' with them. But they never did, and when I got my first recommendation on our local community group, Marlow Parents, it absolutely made my day!

My business was a slow burner, it needed to be, because I could not have managed, energetically or physically with it being anything else. I realise that now, and at that point, I had no desire for it to do any more than trickle in a small bit of income which would give us the opportunity to go out for a meal or pay for a treat at the weekend. It felt good to be able to do that.

Then my boys got older, my energy started to come back, and I started to think more about what I could do to actually grow this business. Remember, at this time we were in the very early days of social media. When I had my first son in 2006 we still had dial-up internet! That is how rapidly technology has grown, expanded and changed.

So, I happened to find a webinar by a lady who had an expertise in marketing, and in this free webinar she talked about several things, one of which was the value of 'niching' your business. I had always been resistant to any mention of this in the past, because to me it equalled a smaller pot of clients to reach and treat. But the logic of it actually made sense.

If I was able to become a 'specialist' in one area of my reflexology practice, I could target all my efforts into one direction, instead of doing what this lady called 'spray and pray' marketing, putting it out there, closing your eyes (metaphorically) and seeing what comes back. I could totally see the sense in that although it was too scary to start with, so I just put a pregnancy specific page onto my website and left it at that.

It's funny how when you start to focus on one specific area, they are the clients who appear at your door. Over the coming months I focused my efforts into the pregnancy specific area of the reflexology market and found that these were the people requesting treatments. It also narrowed down who I wanted to connect with - people who ran similar businesses to mine and who also focused on pregnancy and birth. It was lovely being able to network with these businesses and people and make new connections.

I never realised that what helps build your business is actually getting out there and talking to people.

Seems obvious, really, doesn't it? But when you are at home waiting for that enquiry email or the phone to ring, it isn't always straightforward. When nothing came through I automatically reversed it on myself. It meant that nobody wanted me to treat them, I wasn't 'good enough'. This wasn't a good or helpful path to go down at this early stage of my career as a therapist as it made me more despondent and less confident that my belief in building this thriving therapy business was going to work.

That is where the networking, both on and offline was my saving grace. It came at exactly the right time to give my confidence a boost, swapping treatments and experiences really helped, and also having people who gave you a bit of accountability, and cheering you on and wanting you to succeed. I realised that how much interest I had in my treatments was almost directly correlated to how much effort I had put in to talking about my business, both on and offline.

Social media, at this point was still a misnomer to me, and I still didn't really understand its mechanism and benefits to any great degree. However, communicating with people from all over the country, some of whom were therapists, and some weren't, felt immensely gratifying.

The first time I invested £100 in an online marketing programme I was terrified. It felt like a huge amount of money, but I had quickly recognised that I couldn't do this thing on my own. I was an expert in my therapy field of reflexology but not in marketing or promotions. What on earth was all that about? Creating my own website was a massive learning journey, and even that had been changed radically since learning about the importance of 'niching' and talking to the customer you want to talk to. Mine at this stage was the stressed, pregnant woman who needed some time out to relax and prepare for the birth of her baby. The more I immersed myself into this specific area, the easier I found it to write about what I did and how I did it, providing examples along the way.

One of my biggest successes in these early days of entering the marketing world was a collaboration with a photographer, an antenatal teacher and a massage therapist, when we organised a Mother's Day competition for pregnant women. This really raised interest in all our services, plus we received the contact details of these women who we were then able to offer tasters of our services to. One of these ladies from 2013 is still my client today.

All these efforts took time and patience. Setting up a therapy business, for me, was not an overnight success, it was a continual evolution of reviewing, reflecting and looking at how I was working.

A lot of my time and energies were taken up looking after my two young boys - as it should be - but I did start to devote more of my spare time to looking at ways to expand my business. Frankly, I stopped sitting on my bum and waiting for the bookings to flood in and I kept going out to find opportunities.

I was still working part-time too, and so life was very busy and not always fulfilling. If I am honest, a lot of the time, reflexology slipped to the bottom of the pile. It felt like just one more thing to 'do'. I was still learning though and despite my lack of energy to focus on the business side of my work, I still loved giving treatments and meeting the variety of different people who came through my treatment room door.

I finally decided to take the plunge and really immerse myself in the pregnancy field about six months into my 'niching' journey by training as a hypnobirthing teacher. I loved my reflexology but craved some variety in what I could offer my clients, and hypnobirthing dovetailed amazingly well with reflexology.

As a result, I trained and set up my courses for couples, teaching them how to use hypnobirthing techniques to build a calm and positive outlook about their birth.

This was a rocky road for me.

I was not your run of the mill, *'I had an amazing hypnobirth therefore I decided to become a teacher'* kind of person. I was someone who had developed a specialist interest in hypnobirthing as a result of what I already did as a reflexologist, and wanted to interpret it and use it in a way which best fit my business.

I was trained in a 'brand' of teaching a certain way, the so-called 'cookie cutter' approach. Every part of my being did not like teaching a course exactly how it was laid out, within a set timeframe, with no training in actually how to teach couples, or manage group dynamics etc.

I struggled with this from day one, but thought I was just being rebellious and uncooperative (yes, I labelled myself)! At this point I had not developed the confidence to actually just do what I wanted without being worried about sticking to the 'formula'.

I realise now that I am not a formula kinda girl!

Looking back, I realise that this was my individuality screaming to emerge, but at that time of being new to this world of hypnobirthing, I felt more constrained and wanted to get it 'right'. These foundations did stand me in extremely good stead and were helpful in the early days of learning and expanding my knowledge, but it did absolutely nothing to help my confidence in building my therapy business.

I spent all summer after training in hypnobirthing writing the course I needed to teach, incorporating all the elements and principles, but making it my own. I had a background in training, so the delivery didn't scare me, I love speaking to people and getting to know them, but I needed to know my subject well before I did that.

When my first couple booked on after a word of mouth recommendation I was absolutely petrified. The idea of teaching hypnobirthing had actually become a reality! I remember the night before so vividly. I told my husband I couldn't do it, I was giving up. I felt sick, so nervous, and all I wanted to do was crawl under the covers and hide!

Safe to say, what we imagine is going to happen in our mind when we are anxious, is highly unlikely to become our reality! Everything went very well, and resulted in a happy couple who brought me flowers at the end of the course.

So herein commenced my hypnobirthing teaching journey, which took many guises and formats, and I was always, always learning.

I often faced my own blocks to me being 'good enough' to teach. I wasn't a midwife, I hadn't done a three-year course to be an antenatal teacher, how could I have the knowledge and expertise to do this? The answer I always came back to was this (and it took a while!) I was willing and able to spend time with others, listen to them and understand their needs. I did not, and would not ever, lace my opinions and views on them,

I would give them the information which enabled them to make the decision which was right for them and inspire their own confidence and self-belief.

That was when I realised this felt good, and right. I was a catalyst to building others' confidence, dispelling myths about hypnobirthing (of which there were many) and helping people realise the actual realities of giving birth - not just what they had heard, or seen, or read. This felt much more within my capabilities and it also meant that I was able to teach the way I wanted to teach.

I am going to skip back a minute here, as something has just occurred to me.

In the early days of qualifying as a reflexologist, I knew I had to embrace Continuing Professional Development (CPD) to 'maintain' my registration with a professional body. By nature I am a person who loves learning new things and expanding my knowledge, and this led me to completing a pregnancy reflexology course to ensure I knew and understood this specialist area fully.

This kind of learning helped me massively in my knowledge and understanding, but it did not make me a 'better' therapist.

What I mean by that is that I already had all the qualities I needed which lent themselves to the therapy I had chosen, listening skills, the ability to communicate and build rapport. These are the things which come from experience in life, not from doing a qualification, and in my opinion, cannot be taught to any great degree but enhanced by our own self-reflection and personal development.

No amount of courses were going to make me a 'better' therapist, I know that now, and so the additional, nonspecific courses I went on, hot stone reflexology, vertical reflex therapy did not inspire me in the same way. Although I did learn a few new techniques, they did not really give me new knowledge or understanding which I incorporated into my everyday practice. In fact, by doing these courses I was actually spreading myself more thinly, having to diversify what I already offered and trying to please different groups of people who would be drawn to different aspects of my work.

That may sound bizarre, but my observation is that those who are always training and learning new skills (myself included) are not always comfortable with who they are and what they offer.

Why digress? Because I now believe that this is what I was doing with hypnobirthing.

I chose it because it complemented what I was already doing in the main pregnancy reflexology and it felt like a good fit. Did I choose it because I thought I was going to love it? No, not really, not when I made the decision.

I fell in love with the concept and principles after I had trained, and started to teach some amazing, inspirational couples but not when I actually made the choice.

It was, however, the right choice for me at that stage of my journey, and I loved it for that reason. It enabled me to grow in confidence about my offering, and led to me spending more time setting up this new aspect of my business.

One thing I continually craved during these early years as a therapist and teacher was supportive groups with whom I could work with and alongside. I was still working part-time and it was beginning to be a struggle to balance all aspects of my business, and look after my boys. I was finding myself working, doing the 'mum thing' then going out to teach or see reflexology clients in the evening. It was exhausting and, looking back, I am not really sure how I managed it.

The reason I believed I kept going was because I wanted to do something more with my life. I didn't just want to be employed. I wanted flexibility and the opportunity to support people in a way I had never been able to before.

I suppose I should mention at this point that in my early career I was a social worker. For 14 years I worked with vulnerable groups in our society, those who were often pigeon-holed and marginalised, and only really came to the fore following a tragic child death, when the public and the media would scrutinise and blame the social workers for 'failing' and 'getting it all wrong'.

I was one of those professionals who sat in the thick of all that crap, where people forgot we were human too, and that, unfortunately, when we operate within a bureaucratic, money-led organisation, tragic mistakes happen with peoples' lives. It is never one person's fault, but don't we just love to have a scapegoat?

I was passionate about supporting these people, and in my early twenties, bent over backwards to try and give my families some understanding and practical help to help them move forward. It is not an easy job and I witnessed and dealt with some horrendous stuff, including threats to my life.

I didn't realise how vulnerable I was until, at the age of 25, I nearly had a nervous breakdown. I was burnt-out, frightened and overwhelmed, and I had no idea what was happening to me. Eventually I left the organisation I was in, before it broke me, and I moved to work within the charitable sector, which I loved. It was still, however, a place which could drain your energy, and creating a work/life balance was incredibly difficult. When you are a newly married woman with a husband who works full-time that doesn't seem to matter, but when you are pregnant with your first child, everything seems to shift in perspective.

I wanted to go back and work for this charity more than anything else. I loved it. I thought that because it was a children's charity it would be compatible with having children, but I was wrong.

Unfortunately, the need to give yourself over entirely to a job which supported people, especially vulnerable people was a given, whether you worked in the local authority or charitable sector. So I had to make the heart-wrenching decision to leave this job whilst on maternity leave. My baby son was my absolute priority and I was not prepared to compromise and return to full-time work. It didn't feel right. I think this experience led me to realise how important these boundaries are when you a parent.

When I got offered a part-time job working for a local Fostering and Adoption Team, I held a caseload which equalled some of the full-time workers. Sometimes I couldn't make meetings or training sessions, but I was always laser focused when I was at work and my clients were 100% supported. On the days I didn't work, I was committed to making sure that the time I spent with Joseph was his time, and not me torn in two trying to do both.

This was my theme of early motherhood - trying to work out the best possible way to be a mum, enjoy his babyhood (and my job) and be me, whilst bringing in an income at the same time.

When I brought my therapies into the mix, it did complicate things for quite a while. I became a juggler extraordinaire, and at every spare moment I'd find myself trying to fit something in, whether it was a work appointment, seeing a client or meeting up with friends so the boys could spend time with their baby friends. What I didn't really factor into my time was self-care. I didn't realise you had to at this point, so I just kept running around the hamster wheel which is life.

My therapy business continued to tick over. I realise now that the 'ticking over' was because I was spreading my energies far and wide. In one day I could go from helping find a respite placement for a vulnerable child with foster parents, to refereeing a fight between my two boys, feeding and getting them to bed, and then meeting with a client with chronic stress who needed time to relax and recharge!

Somehow, in my infinite wisdom, I decided to add something else to the mix and began assessing Foster carers for a private company. More independent work meant even more juggling. Looking back now my schedule must have been crazy. Some of my friends would often say to me "I don't know how you do it" and this would trigger something in me – I'd get defensive. I used to think, well it's okay for you because you don't have to work, you don't have the challenges of earning an income etc. I know now that my pissed-off-ness is because there was a grain of truth in what they were saying, I was doing too much and overstretching myself massively, to the point of absolute overwhelm. My body and my brain were ever expanding to try to cope. But it couldn't carry on like that forever.

My capacity to cope was reaching breaking point when my close friend was fighting breast cancer. I desperately wanted to be there for her, support her in whatever way I could. The previous year another friend had died after a short battle with cancer, and this brought everything into a very sharp focus for me. It scared me into realising that we couldn't take our body, or lives for granted, and chronic stress, and pushing would only work for so long. It was around this time that I became self- employed and took up a small part-time contract with a local charity, using my expertise, but on my terms.

I felt so much more in control of my work, I managed my diary completely and got the job done efficiently and with so much less stress than working within a bureaucratic organisation. I loved the team I worked with, and there wasn't the 'burnout and work at all costs' ethic I'd experienced at the last charity I worked for, and it went some way to supporting me at a time when I actually needed time with others, and emotional support. It also gave me the opportunity to focus on growing what was becoming a thriving therapy practice.

Since the day of volunteering to be the reflexologist at an indulgence evening, my client base had grown, and word of mouth was my absolute best form of marketing.

I worked soundly and ethically, I kept within what I knew and became very confident within my field. I did expand my knowledge, but I did not believe I needed new skills or new ways of doing things.

I often felt that when I went on some training courses we were often being taught that their way to do it was the best way, instead of trying to adapt the method to suit our own skills as therapists. There was also a bit of a competitive element too which I totally hated. I know now, so strongly, that people buy people and at the end of the day, if you have not got that rapport, nothing else really matters.

I ended up discarding the courses I'd done previously, or adapting the skills to suit me, and I kept well away from courses which advocated prescribed protocols. That's why I fell out of love with the brand of hypnobirthing I'd trained in. The course outline had said it wasn't prescriptive, but it was, and this didn't suit my style of teaching or my proven ability to build confidence in others, however they were feeling.

I just couldn't teach a prescriptive course, or deal with others who couldn't take the honesty of feeling your own way. When you are a social worker you are taught to assess a situation, and take an approach based on what is needed. This is not what I believed my therapy training or teaching offered, and I couldn't really find a forum to truly share this without feeling criticised or judged.

I have to say, it has taken me a long time to confidently get to this point, and to rise up and honour this feeling. It is not in any way coming from a place of dislike about something, or how other people chose to run their classes or their businesses, it was based on me, working in a way I felt comfortable (ethically and professionally of course). It was about doing things my way, based on my experience both as a social worker and in other capacities supporting vulnerable families, and as a therapist, treating and supporting the people who came through my door.

My point is, once I realised that I was not the product of my qualifications, that they didn't define what I did, it was being me that defined what I did, everything else seemed to feel so much easier.

I stopped getting upset at others' comments that I should be teaching hypnobirthing within a certain time framework otherwise it wasn't hypnobirthing. I stopped worrying that I wasn't finding enough out on peoples' feet to make their treatment worthwhile (yes in the early days I did think this). I was totally undervaluing myself and other peoples' right to have an opinion about what they were experiencing, and how the treatments left them feeling, and just loaded myself with self-judgement - not a good place to be!

My reflexology repeat clientele and my word of mouth recommendations, as well as people coming back for subsequent births, should have been enough of a message that I was doing a good job, that people received what they needed from me when I supported them. But, unfortunately, it wasn't, because I didn't truly believe in myself, I didn't have full confidence in myself and my abilities.

I thought a great deal about this and came to the conclusion that a lot of this was to do with my experience in my early professional career. Much of what I did wasn't good enough. People were quick to criticise and judge, and I was so used to this approach that when I worked as a therapist I was almost waiting for the negative comments, the criticism, the feedback that I wasn't getting it right for people.

When you actually think about this logically, what could I be doing wrong? I was well trained in my field, I worked very much on the principle of empowering people to find their own way, their own solutions whilst providing information, support and guidance. My treatments were an 'experience' an opportunity for people to receive something positive which they needed at that moment.

I truly believe that the reason therapists go on a journey of perpetual training is not for CPD necessarily, it is often because they 'don't feel good enough', and they need that external ratification for their own confidence and self-belief.

The thing is, though, and what I have learnt, is that you could have 100 people telling you how amazing you are, but unless you believe it yourself, no person, training, or qualification is going to make you feel better, it certainly didn't for me.

I might be saying these things now, but whilst building my therapy business I spent a lot of time battling these feelings. I have always been an outspoken person, with opinions (my husband usually hides when I get going). However, I was spouting hot air out at the world to cover up my own insecurities and uncertainties about what I was doing, and the fact that I didn't feel comfortable with just being myself in my business. Yes, I needed the knowledge my qualifications gave me, but at this point I hadn't really stepped into who I was as a therapist. I was keeping firmly behind the 'I'm a reflexologist' or 'I'm a hypnobirthing teacher' brand of thinking without really feeling comfortable with either.

Why am I writing all this? Because I believe it will save other therapists so much time, effort and money if they could take a big step back and recognise what they really need to successfully grow the business they have a desire to grow.

Is it to do with having more qualifications, or is it to do with actually feeling comfortable in our own skins, with what we offer, and feeling comfortable with that?

Success

...ade a difference to me, and helped ...to grow and evolve into being the ...I am today? Before I go into this I want to say that that we never stop growing, experiencing and learning. This book is a product of all my experiences to date, but I know that I am going to have so many more along the way, some expected and some not so much!

So, I was this therapist, with regular clientele but I still had the wish, this desire in me to do and grow more. I had come to realise that it wasn't about the weekend course which taught me how to be a 'better' therapist, it was actually about how I could learn about me, and what was stopping me doing what I truly wanted to do, which was to continue to thrive, and grow.

I also had a family to support, I was still working part-time and by now, my boys had started school. This prompted me to leave social work and become a self-employed practitioner for this local charity. In doing so, I had the flexibility to do what I absolutely needed, and wanted to do (take, my boys to and from school every day, be there for them when they came home and be physically and emotionally available to them when they got home).

You see, that was what was missing when I worked as a social worker. I gave my all to my job because I truly wanted to make a difference in peoples' lives, but at the end of the day, when I came home I was mentally and physically drained, and I just couldn't enjoy being with my children as much as I wanted to. Hands up here, I struggled to be patient with them, I lost my temper and then I felt incredibly, incredibly guilty because they are my priority. But I felt completely wrung out, as if there was nothing left of me to enjoy being with them, to see the world through their eyes, to listen and understand.

This is the working mum side people don't often see, the bit where we try desperately to be all things to all people, and end up doing a half-arsed job everywhere, and feeling rubbish about it. Or, we bend over backwards to make sure everyone else's needs are met, and deplete ourselves to the point that there is nothing left for us to fall back on, to allow us the time and space we desperately need.

I truly believed that my therapy business was my opportunity to create the space to be me, as well as being able to be emotionally present for my boys. I was beyond exhausted, but I didn't recognise it at this point. I just kept on going, and going, and going, until one day my husband asked me to leave the house and go and take some time on my own. He was concerned that my emotional outbursts – crying, getting angry and upset for seemingly no reason - were negatively impacting on the boys. I fought against this to start with, but he has always been so open and honest with me that eventually, when I had stopped fighting against what he was saying, and calmed down, I began to realise he was right.

At the time, I recognised that although I had reduced my hours with my self-employed role for a charity, I was slotting in every hour with other work, foster carer assessments and my business as a therapist and teacher. I realise now that I was doing this because I was scared, scared that if I didn't keep it all going, keep filling in the gaps with work, then the money would stop flowing in, so I had to keep busy.

The absolute irony was, that I was now busier and more frantic than when I had one social work position and my therapy business, because I was now trying to juggle several independent roles! When I look back now I have absolutely no idea how I managed everything, really, absolutely no idea. I look at my old diaries and see the appointments and me scooting here there and everywhere and I cannot believe that I just substituted one emotional drain for another.

I look back now with clarity, but at the time I felt I was doing the best for me, and my family. However, I also had a personal life too, a friend who was fighting cancer, a growing family whose needs were changing every day. As my boys grew I truly felt they needed me more in some ways than they had when they were younger. They needed me to be present and to help them negotiate the ups and downs of school life.

So, what was I doing with all the business stuff in the background?

I was starting to:

- learn about the practical aspects of growing, and marketing a business

- listen to webinars in the evening and connecting with more and more entrepreneurial business women online.

How did this make a difference?

It helped me see I was not alone in my endeavours, that there were other women out there struggling to achieve the work/life balance that I was.

I found that groups of the 'same' therapists, reflexologists, hypnobirthing teachers were all on their own journey, and when I often connected, and tried to build relationships with them, there was often a sense of unease and competitiveness, which I didn't like. I recognised it because it was in me too, and this made me feel uncomfortable, so I tended to spend time getting to know a variety of different business women and avoiding groups where there was a 'my way is the best way' mentality.

It took me a year to close that door to the social work arena. I wanted to stop working for the charity and knew I needed to decide between running a business I loved, and a profession, which I had given my all to for 15 years. I was ready to break free in my heart, but my head kept me securely latched on through fear. Again, all those scary messages were flying through my head. What if I couldn't make enough money to sustain 'just' running my own business? What if I failed?

I neglected to see all the evidence in front of me, at that point: the eight years in practice, the ongoing referrals and enquiries, and the trying to fit people in so I could juggle it all.

But I hung on, I raised my hourly rate at the charity, almost as a test to see if they still wanted me, and they did. I tried to value myself through doing this, but the money wasn't really the issue at that point, it was my time.

So, what did I do in a situation where I was struggling to get everything done, meet my clients' needs, continue to grow my business and remain in a profession which could be exceptionally demanding at times? I started studying! Mad? Looking back now I can say absolutely that I was beyond nuts. But in that moment, I was so full of fear of what the future might hold and that if I remained steady in my business with 'just' the qualifications I had, it would not keep or sustain me or my family.

I had such a poverty mindset at this point, a real fear of lack, and I was continually predicting the future around what 'might' go wrong instead of what was, amazingly continuing to go right.

I was always living in the future in my head, looking to the next month, the next client, the next opportunity that I failed to see what I had in the present moment.

Isn't that so common? While we are giving it our all in whatever we choose to do, we always have an eye on the prize at some point in our future, and we never celebrate where we actually are. So there I was, raising a thriving family who I loved with all my heart. I was fulfilling my passion of supporting couples and individuals, helping to build confidence and address issues during pregnancy, birth and beyond. But still I had this desire to do something more.

I continued to look outward though, and decided that a hypnotherapy course was the way to go after considering what would dovetail nicely into my business and successfully expand my knowledge. However, after completing this year-long course, the results were unexpected and profound. I loved the course, somehow managed to fit my case studies into my amazingly and ridiculously tight schedule, and I started to feel less fearful of leaving my self-employed role within the social work arena. I started to see this as a possibility, rather than something to fear.

By the time I made the decision, six months into my hypnotherapy course, I was there in my head as well as in my heart.

It felt effortless because I stopped thinking about what could go wrong and started thinking about what could go right.

I was amazed by my mindset change, and although I had my wobbles (I wouldn't be human if I didn't) I finally said goodbye to working in an organisation in March 2015.

There were no fanfares, no big hurrahs, just the end of an era for me. It was bittersweet because the last 'team' I worked with at the charity were my absolute best team of all, after working with hundreds of people throughout my career. They are the only group I remain in touch with and I miss them all as individuals and what we did when we came together.

What I didn't miss was being part of someone else's organisational structure, I wanted to create my own structure, in my own way.

At that time, I had no idea how this was going to evolve, but something had happened to me during my hypnotherapy experience and this part of my future felt clearer and brighter than it ever had been.

This was a fantastic move forward professionally, but as us entrepreneurs know, when we work solely following our dreams and passions to do what we love, our business and personal lives are totally intertwined.

In the background, and the foreground of all of this, my beautiful friend was losing her six-year battle with cancer. I was doing everything I could, practically, and emotionally to support her, give her my love and healing whenever I could. This experience was one of the saddest, and most profound I have had to date, and when I finally had to say goodbye to her in June 2015, I never thought the journey could get any harder than this.

However, my strengths and skills in my business after she died, also became my greatest weakness and vulnerability.

I missed her terribly, the feeling and hole she left was like nothing I had ever experienced.

But, I was a therapist, I could cope, I knew how to cope, so I could 'therapy' my way out of this grief. How wrong was I?

Not only was I not able to think myself through this, I almost dug myself in deeper by immersing myself in what I had always been good at, study and academic achievement. So, for the first six weeks after she died I wrote and completed my hypnotherapy diploma. The plan was that following this I would add to my plethora of skills, a thriving therapy practice. I was leaning heavily on a variety of coaches and coaching solutions at the time, believing that the answers and the suggestions they gave me were what I needed to grow this amazing, diverse therapy practice. Wrong again!

The more I pushed to get things going, the more it all seemed to slow down. The more I tried to start, and complete tasks related to the successful marketing and awareness raising of my business, the more it seemed to stagnate. Until I was paralysed.

I was doing what I could to tick through the early months after her death, but that was all I could manage. Grief is a strange emotion, it sort of creeps up on you until it is part of your everyday life. It is a feeling you have to learn to live with, and it can catch you out at the most unexpected of times. I lost a lot of my drive, ambition and perspective at this time and essentially felt very lost.

I thought that hiring a variety of different coaches would help me through, but as soon as I tried to move forward I collapsed in another emotional heap, or my insecurities started creeping in, that fear of the future, what might go wrong, I'm not good enough, capable enough, skilled enough, I felt like I was continually back at square one.

During this difficult period, I very nearly, several times, gave up on my business. Why? It just became too hard to see a way through. I was getting up in the morning, seeing clients, and in-between sitting staring at a computer screen willing for some amazing motivation to come forth to grow and evolve this business which I promised myself that I would have.

I started to bargain with myself, if I watched an hour of a box set, I would do an hour of work, whatever that was. I found that I was willing the programme not to end and when it did I would sit and cry, not wanting to go and do anything. I wanted to just sit and do nothing.

I totally beat myself up about this, completely and utterly. I was my own worst critic and enemy - as I think we all are most of the time. I would not, somehow, could not let myself stop and just do absolutely nothing. I had to keep on going, and pushing and pretending that everything was okay. I have some lovely friends, most of whom I have met and made since becoming a parent, and they all wanted me to do well in my business.

Their most common question when seeing me was 'are you busy?' which was their way of intending to enquire after the success, or failure, of my business. The bizarre, ironic thing was, I was busy, but I was also breaking down inside. My business was thriving, I was doing my reflexology and teaching my hypnobirthing. I preserved what little energy I had for these times to support my clients to the best of my ability. Outside of those times though I was flat as a pancake, very little energy of any kind or zest for life. What hurt the most was that I did not know who I could talk to, turn to, when I was in this place.

The enormity of my beautiful friend dying and leaving behind a nine year-old daughter had scared a lot of people. It was real, it could happen, and a number of my friends found it difficult to talk about. This is not a criticism of those people in any way, shape or form, they were on their own journey, and had their own way of dealing with things.

But talking was the way I coped, how I moved through this intense period of grieving, and missing my friend. I wanted to talk, about her, about how amazing she was, I could not just stop talking about her after the funeral. I had made a promise to her that I would look out for and support her daughter, and my husband was also supporting her grieving husband. These were dark, difficult times where we found it hard to face the reality of the situation sometimes. I found it so immensely difficult to go into their home to start with, there was a big space where she wasn't physically there anymore and that was so hard to take.

My husband was amazing at this time, we shared a lot about our own journey with this and I believe it brought us closer together. I loved him that little bit more the day he told me he had researched online about supporting a grieving husband because he so wanted to be there for his friend too. We learnt not to take anything for granted and he reflected to me how I really was.

I was depressed and in a low mood - a reaction to such an immensely difficult situation which I had absolutely no control over. I could not just 'lift' my way out of my grief. Grief is most definitely a journey which I have absolutely experienced.

You have to learn to speak and say things which people don't want to hear or say themselves. Speaking is okay. I turned to people who could cope with my outpouring because they understood the grieving process, or were able to recognise that these emotions were mine, not theirs.

Although I wouldn't have wished this experience or devastation on anyone, I would give everything to have my beautiful friend back with us, I believe grief's hidden gift was the understanding and empathy I was able to provide for my clients. My understanding of emotional rawness and desperation deepened - those times when you really can't see the wood for the trees, and you are stuck somewhere so deep and fearful you feel like you will never have the strength to climb out.

I have been there, I thought that this deep grieving process was never going to end, this journey of looking for the answers and pushing my way through. It took me a year before I finally stopped battling and gave in to what my body, and mind had been demanding that I do: stop, rest, switch off and just let everything start flowing in the way it needed to, (whichever way that was).

I spent much of that time cherishing my family. They had come into sharp focus during this most important, and significant period of my life.

I learnt that you didn't need to keep doing to move forward, that actually stopping and letting go was much more effective when it came to growing my business.

Sounds counter-intuitive? I totally get that, it really did to me, but I kept seeing signs that when I did stop, and do nothing (and by nothing, I mean doing things I wanted and needed to do) I would find that my appointments would book up. The loveliest of clients would come wanting support, and the time and energy I continued to put back into my business started to heal my heart.

This was not an easy, straightforward journey, and in no way could I give you a magic formula which tells you how to do it. Grief is such an intensely personal thing, where everything about you comes into sharp focus, all your insecurities and vulnerabilities. I had to move through it, and these are the people and therapies I used to help me do that.

EFT, Emotional Freedom Technique

This was an absolute godsend to me. I didn't realise it at the time, but when my business coach told me that nothing would happen in my business until I sorted out my emotional health, I eventually had to accept that this was the absolute truth. In my head it was not 'another avenue where I had to talk to someone about my stuff'. Even though I am an analytical person and love to talk things through, it was getting harder and harder to talk through the tough stuff because it was so tough.

When I spoke to an EFT practitioner what she said made sense, but I was also guarded about how it would really help me in my everyday life. However, I needed to do something, I was wary of the 'having a coach' obsession which I seemed to have taken on. At one point in 2016 I found myself working with three different coaches with three different perspectives, and it was messing with my head! What I know now, is that I was looking for other people to find the answers for me. I was avoiding the fact that I needed to look within and stop modelling myself on how other people saw me and thought I should be.

EFT did the looking within without one shadow of a doubt. I crashed in a big way and it was a really scary time for me. I remember one session where my practitioner (who was doing the therapy via skype) had to talk to me as I had my head on the desk while I sobbed my heart out. I was angry with her for getting the time of our call wrong, feeling desperate for someone to come and take this pain away. I did not know how to cope but felt I should cope because I was a therapist who supported others with their emotions and experiences, how wrong was I?!

I fell into another black hole which I wasn't expecting, I thought I had done all the healing that I needed to do after my friend's death, I was 'sorted', I could move on with growing my business. Wrong again. What I had done was address the first step on the journey. I had moved forward, but not as far as I had thought. It was an immensely difficult time for me, and for those around me as I identified and discovered that I needed to work on, and heal my relationship with my mum. Cliché? It felt a bit like that at the time, but I had to do something, and through the wonders of EFT I had got to the root cause of my issues.

This relationship was not my mum's responsibility, it was mine, and how I responded to it. It is a whole other book to go into this story, it is a painful process with a lot of reality checks and realisation that I am an adult, I can truly do what I want, but it sunk me into the depths of despair again. I had no energy, I was flat again whilst trying to parent my children and maintain some semblance of normality. And all around me people continued to ask me if I was busy, and tell me how fortunate I was to be able to run my own business. Inside I just felt like shouting, "It's not easy, it's not fortunate, it's the toughest thing I have ever done because it is not about the clients, it is not about the income, it is how it forces you to look at yourself and why you behave the way you do. Your confidence, your self-belief, the way you respond and react to others, what drains your energy, what overwhelms you, and what stops you being productive."

The thing is, if running a business was easy, then everyone would be doing it. If running a business was just simply about telling people what you did and them booking appointments was all it took then I would be happy, but it isn't.

I had regular clients and a lovely group of people using and recommending my services. When I was working in my business I was in flow, it felt awesome and I could seriously do it all day, every day. However, when I tried to work 'on' my business, that is when the struggles emerged. I'd continually end up in a heap when I tried to get something done but it just wasn't happening. Most of the time I would sit there not actually knowing what to do or how to do it. I'd just stare at a blank screen and an endless to-do list.

What was the actual 'formula' for growing these 100K businesses which these seemingly 'normal' mums with children

were growing? I had no idea.

I signed up for toolkits, printed off blueprints, and all the time I felt like I was just going through the motions, checking off the lists to make my business thrive. Online course production, passive income, they were all buzz words which promised me an opportunity to have more free time to spend with my children and more money in my bank account. But what about if I actually wanted to spend time with clients, get to know them and work with them on a one-to-one way? I struggled to fit my head around what I was 'supposed' to be doing to grow my business with what I actually wanted to do, and I was in this tug of war between heart and head (again) for a long while.

In the background I was 'working' on myself, continuing the EFT and having energy healing to deal with energetic blocks which kept coming up because I was spending so much time looking within instead of looking to other people to sort out my business for me. I have had so many false starts with coaches, so many I didn't even finish working with, who just drifted into and out of my life, I never really knew what I received from them. However, I did not realise that every single coach I worked with helped me masses. They helped me to see where I was, where I was going and what I no longer needed. So, when I let one of the relationships go, I had to turn it on its head to help me see what was good about that relationship, and how it had truly helped and guided me.

My lovely husband was doing his thing in the corporate world, and he'd let me just get on with my stuff, even though at times it really laid me low. I truly believe that's why people often walk away from therapeutic intervention, even midway through, because most of the time it certainly gets worse before it gets better.

My EFT teacher taught me that. I seriously had to hang on for what was, and still is a rollercoaster of a ride. The difference is that the ups, and the downs are not so extreme now, the stomach clenching moments do not last nearly as long, and I have more tools, and more confidence to enable me to move myself out of them in an empowering and an 'I've got this' kinda way.

A major learning point for me was realising that I needed to be open to other therapies to keep myself healing and getting into a better and better place to continue to build and grow a business which would thrive, even when I was not at my best.

This also meant letting go of friendships and relationships which no longer served me or my life, even though at the time I had received immense benefit from them.

One particular experience taught me about not putting others up on pedestals, even when they have guided and influenced your life in a positive and significant way. I am always very clear to clients and to people in my everyday life that we all have our 'human moments' and these people, however highly regarded and valued they are, do too.

That was a major shock to the system when someone who'd had a profound influence on my life and my spiritual journey behaved in a way which I believe was not congruent with her teachings or what she represented. I felt powerless to do anything about it at the time, and massively let down. Safe to say it was a real lesson to me that I was not and could not rely on anyone else but myself on this journey to building this business and working on me. The other people in my life were just there to hold my hand and be support, but were not the definition of my experience. These were not cheap lessons financially.

The investment I continued to put into my business did not always realise a financial return. I believe, though, that even if I hadn't been running a business I would have needed to invest in myself financially in some way, so I could not and would not turn away from this personal investment in my business.

I remember my accountant saying during a year-end meeting, "if you didn't pay out for all this business coaching you would be further in profit". I got where she was coming from, but I also believed that I would not be where I was if I hadn't actually invested in myself and my business in the first place!

In amongst all this personal introspection and what some would term 'navel gazing' I was beginning to fall in love with my business and what it represented for me.

Over the course of the past 11 years I had gathered a variety of domain names and business identities. This included one for my reflexology and one for my hypnobirthing business. Then, when I qualified as a hypnotherapist, I realised that neither fitted this new tool.

What to do? Another Facebook page? Another website? I wasn't keeping on top of the ones I had so I did not believe that was the way to go, it would create more work than I was prepared to handle. What this did was create an opportunity for me, which originally, I looked upon as a headache.

The opportunity was related to me actually becoming me, and not a number of therapy specific Facebook pages and domain names I had become. So, instead of remaining as 'Marlow Reflexology' and 'Blissful Birthing', which were my two business names, I became myself, clarecogan.com. How absolutely self-centred was that?

A website and Facebook page which spoke all about me, was all about me! I struggled to let go of Marlow Reflexology as this had been my identity for so long. I knew from a business perspective it ticked all the right boxes, it heighted my SEO rankings, I was easy to find, people contacted me regularly through doing the good old 'Google search'. But, as I had grown into myself, and my confidence was increasing, I found that I had outgrown this name and grown into myself.

Blissful Birthing was a spinoff from hypnobirthing because Marlow Reflexology didn't 'fit' hypnobirthing, so that was how I ended up with two of everything. And it did my head in!

Eventually, a Mastermind programme I was working on gave me the impetus, and the courage to merge the two Facebook pages. I had spent so long living in fear that I would 'lose' people if I did this and No one 'would find me'. What happened in reality was that I was able to communicate so much better using one avenue, and the followers I feared I would lose, actually stayed. What also happened was that it gave me an opportunity to change my name, and become me, who I really was. My business was not reflexology, or hypnobirthing, or hypnotherapy, it was what I brought to the sessions, my approach, using my intuition to support and guide people in whatever way was needed at the time. And it felt good for the first time to actually own it, be myself and not a business name, put something there which I could identify with, and not just what I though everyone else wanted to see.

The spinoff from this was the evolution of the way I represented and marketed my business. This was an interesting time where I was still being heavily guided by business coaches whilst I dealt with these profound personal issues. I honestly needed that at this point because I seriously could not see the wood for the trees. One of the introductions was to a graphic designer, Vicki Nicholson, who did 'branding packages' for people (and designed the cover of this book). So, in the past and throughout my business I'd had a number of logos designed, and websites built, but I had never truly looked at my business and how I wanted it to look. I was the same as the majority of people, I just thought it was all about the logo, the design of that logo which would then be put on banners, headers and marketing material. Wrong!

When I spoke to this lady, what she said made perfect sense. Branding is about the look and feel of your business, what represents who you are. In becoming clarecogan.com I had also realised that I needed to reflect all my marketing, on and off line using this personal approach, so rebranding it was. Seriously, it was and has been one of the best investments in my business to date.

Before I started working with her, I was working with a graphic designer from a site called PeoplePerHour, where you hire people to do different projects. They were trying to design a logo for me, but despite numerous explanations and examples, what was in my head was not coming out in any way, shape or form on paper. When I met the lovely Vicki, she spent time actually talking to me and getting to know my business, and what she produced was nothing short of phenomenal. It was about the colours I liked, the fonts which resonated with me, not what I thought others would like and want. And I fell in love with my business a little bit more.

So here I was, with the most beautiful branded business, enabling me to really create eye-catching, creative stuff to capture potential clients and my followers' attention. It reflected who I was more than anything else had ever done and I was finally comfortable with seeing photos of myself incorporated into my branding. I loved it, I truly did, but having gorgeous branding and consistent colours does not make a business, although it certainly enhances it. What I was beginning to find was that I was dragging my heels, again. I was immersed in so many groups and activities. To add to my list, I was running a monthly positive birth group. I had joined the local Maternity Network group which linked birth professionals together to share, support and cross refer, and I was the joint co-ordinator for my local area. I was meeting lots of lovely people, and having referrals made to me by professionals as well as clients. But I was still struggling.

I kept reminding myself that I was 'doing the do', taking guidance and support and transferring it into action, and taking steps in the right direction. However, what I had come to realise was that I wasn't sure what the right direction was, and whether I was making the right choices for me. I say this now, on reflection, because at the time I believed I was ticking all the boxes: I was out there, joining in, not competing, working together with other professionals, providing free support, giving my time freely. But none of it really, truly resonated, and I couldn't understand why.

What I was finding was that everything seemed like a bit of an effort, everything required a new aspect of learning, or an investment of my time. All I kept thinking was that this was okay, this was how it was meant to be, I was growing my business, moving it forward. I did vision boards, I meditated, I was coached, I did what the coaches told me. Don't get me wrong, I did have periods of elation and enjoyment, but most of those times came when I was seeing and treating clients, which is when I really felt like me, and that I was doing what I loved. I was finding that in the networking arena, I was getting really caught up in politics and what I now term 'other peoples' stories', other peoples' interpretation of situations and other peoples' businesses.

It was the kind of politics I had strived to get away from when I left my profession, and it felt like I was being dragged back into it unexpectedly and without realising. This kind of 'talking about others' drained my energy, analysing other peoples' businesses and what they were up to was not what I was about. I didn't want to know how much someone else in my field charged or how qualified they were, but by joining in with these networks I was finding more and more that I was noticing the one-upmanship and competition from other birth-related business owners. I know now that this was their stuff, their insecurities about their business, and their lack of willingness to really embrace the true spirit of working together. Sounds harsh? Well to be honest it was harsh, I needed to protect my time, space and boundaries to be with people who were going to work with me and lift me up, so that I could reciprocate that support, not pay lip service to supporting one another.

During my 11 years as a therapist I have come across many many therapists, they come and go, some stick around, but not many. They have replicated parts of my website, taken my business names (which they had every right to as they were not trademarked) and generally just tried to lift themselves up using my identity.

At first it used to really annoy and preoccupy me, these were people who had used my hard work to benefit their business. Not fair, right? But do you know what, as I have grown and emerged into the business owner I am today, I hold very little time for these people and don't give them my attention. If other therapists want to undercut my prices so that clients who have come to me initially start using their services, that's fine. If people want to replicate what I do, then that is equally fine.

Don't get me wrong, this perspective did not happen in any way, shape or form overnight, but I have learnt to put my time, and energy where I choose it to be rather than where I think it should be.

This was the time in my business when I really wanted to drive it forward, I wanted it to grow, and thrive. Everything was in place, people were there to help me, so why couldn't I get it going? Things often felt like a false start to me, three steps forward, five back, and I couldn't figure out what was going on, or why it was happening.

Let's focus on my website to give one such example of how my perspective and approach has shifted with my experience.

When I first qualified as a reflexologist I was told, by many that I needed a website. That it was seen as the 'brochure' of my services, showcasing what I could do. I mentioned earlier in this book that this was where I started, getting the website sorted and then sitting back and waiting for the phone to ring (which it didn't, if you remember). This site was a prebuilt one where I just inputted my information. It was a great one for a new starter like me, as I didn't need to embrace myself in all the techie stuff, I just wrote what I needed, used the 'keywords' as the company suggested and paid my monthly fee after choosing my domain name. It totally took all the issues out of my hands, and I loved that as I really didn't have a clue.

At the time this worked, when I look back now I realised that I was actually paying quite a lot of money for a company to do something which did not require much time on their part. That was a massive learning curve for me, it is easy to just hand things over to people when we are not sure what we are doing, to get it done. When you are a newly qualified therapist, or even an existing therapist moving with the times, you want to tick things off the list, the website is always a biggie, and one I got completely hung up on, just as many other therapists have.

Don't get me wrong, a website is important, and the first time someone told me they had 'Googled' me was hilarious, I never imagined I would be found on Google! However, what I found was by handing over control of my site to someone else meant that I was allowing someone else to define the therapist that I was.

If you looked at my site in the early days, I was pretty 'vanilla'. My site looked pretty much the same as every other reflexologist's I could find (and yes I was still doing the searchy thing when I qualified). I talked about me, my qualifications, what reflexology was, what happens during a reflexology treatment and 'how' it worked along with my prices and contact details. There was absolutely nothing to distinguish me from other reflexologists, it would just be literally who this searcher came upon first. All thoughts were about getting to the top of Google so I would be found first. In the early days of Google and searching, that may have worked in my favour, although my cold contacts (people I didn't know) were few and far between. What I know now, 11 years on, is that people are much more discerning, they search around, they look at different things, apply their own criteria to their judgements to make a decision, it is not simply a case of search and click.

I believe that this is because reflexology is so personal, as are hypnotherapy and hypnobirthing, and people have evolved when it comes to using the internet and making selective judgements.

Websites are not about providing an online leaflet about your services, it is now needing to be all about you. Sound vain and egotistical? I totally get that.

So, after about four years of using this pre-packaged company hosting and doing everything for my website, I fell out of love with it, big time. It started to control me around the time I started to learn and understand some key principles of marketing as a therapy business. I really wanted to expand in the directions being taught to me, and understood the value of, but the website could not accommodate my needs. Shortly before I started to flex my web building muscles, they offered me a complete redesign of my website, and colours etc. That was great, didn't it look pretty and therapy like?

But hang on, it doesn't function in the way I need it to. Every time I tried to ask them how I could do things like add a sign-up box so I could run a newsletter and email capture they would pretty much tell me I didn't need it. Very frustrating.

As a therapist, and small business owner, I had to get confident, and fast. If I wanted my business to grow, then I had to be prepared to do things my way, what I felt was right, not how people told me to do it, even my therapy trainers.

So, when I hit this resistance to my website I realised no one was going to make the decision for me. I was going to get out there and get this stuff sorted, based on what I understood worked, and by building a site which reflected my personality and showcased my skills - not create something which was someone else's idea of how to showcase as a therapy business.

I was then incredibly lucky, as, based on a recommendation, I found an amazing web designer and developer. Now, another big learning curve for me here, web designers and web developers are not one and the same thing.

Web designers make sites look pretty, web developers get into the nitty gritty and make things function and work proper. The guy I found could do both, and the designer bits he didn't feel he could manage he contracted out, on my behalf. He totally supported my vision for my reflexology site, as I was actually doing what I needed to do to fill in the gaps - the writing which reflected who I was at that time and what I could offer.

This site was developed around the time I was working very pregnancy specific, and getting other experts to help me in my endeavours. I hired a copywriter to turn my copy into something readable and eye catching, and my web guy put it all together. I have to be honest with you here, as this is what this book is all about, at this time, pretty much every penny I earnt was being put back into the business. I was still working part-time at this point, and that income was paying the bills. I did have flexibility to use this money to do what I knew I needed to do, which was to get the infrastructure in place to get my name, and my business out there.

This stuff was also tangible, it was the 'doing part', a bit like the branding - which was awesome. I loved seeing it all come together and it was very project-based for me. Looking back now I realise that it is easy to get caught up in the creating, and lose sight of the actual doing.

One particular example is a freebie I got a copywriter to create for me, as freebies were a good way to capture emails, right?

Yep, I understood the principle, and it would be a great addition to my newly vamped website, but the thing is with a freebie, you can't put it on your site and

then expect everyone to just sign up, you have to actually tell people about it too!

So many learning curves on this journey, I think I had one sign up on this freebie which probably cost me about £200 to get other people to develop. Sound crazy? Yep likely, but when you are trying to follow others' formula of success and doing what others are guiding you to do, you will pretty much do anything to get it all going.

So many therapists I know have paid thousands for all-singing, all-dancing websites, which they have no idea how to use or amend, and then find themselves held to ransom by their web developer who charges them a fortune every time a small amendment is made, (and not always in a timely fashion).

I, thankfully was not caught in that trap, but I certainly invested heavily in people to help me at this time because I was just not confident enough to do it myself, and that was tough going as I didn't really own what was being produced, even though it was at my direction! So, the story of the website continues. In reality the newly polished site with videos and all sorts of other stuff actually won me a mumpreneur silver award which I was so proud of. This great guy developed my second site too, when I trained as a hypnobirthing teacher, when I was still under the misapprehension that I actually needed one site for every area of my business, because my business names reflected different aspects of it. I look back and realise how time-consuming that all was. I still had the luxury of all my income from my therapies being at my disposal, and I felt like I really indulged this, but not always in the right direction, or for the best return.

None of this I learnt when I trained as a reflexologist, subsequently as a hypnobirthing teacher and then as a hypnotherapist. This was all stuff I learnt through numerous courses I did, hours I spent talking to coaches and lots and lots of reading and video watching. And still I went around in circles!

What people don't tell you when you train to be a therapist and 'set up your business' is that you are everything in that business.

You not only treat people and transform their lives, you also are your accountant, your marketer, your promotions guru, your strategist and your daily operations director. I had some interesting conversations with some of the people I'd trained with, most of whom told me their background was in marketing. I always thought, well that means you are going to be awesome at building this business then. Thing is, not necessarily.

Just because you work in a marketing department of a large organisation, it does not mean you are going to be awesome at marketing your own business. Within an organisation you have one job, one role, and you're part of a team.

When you're marketing your business you see everything through from beginning to end. You make your own daily, and long-term decisions. You are, essentially, your own CEO.

Sound overwhelming? Yes! If someone had explained it like that to me at the beginning of my journey I would have ran for the hills. I was a social worker for goodness sake, my skills were dealing with people, not all this other stuff! And so it continued, me learning how to do stuff I never realised I would need to know. As a therapist I just wanted to do what I was awesome at, help people feel better, and look to others for guidance and support. If someone told me what to do and how to do it, then this business would thrive, right?

The website story over the past 11 years pretty much depicted how I evolved as a therapist, and business owner. Somebody told me I needed headshots to look 'professional' I went out and got headshots done. I hate having my photo taken, and what I recognise now is that sitting there posing for a shot was stilted, it was not me, it was just a reflection of how I thought I needed to be seen in my business.

But, it made me more visible, people could see the real me in amongst the copy which was talking about the difference I make in peoples' lives, not just about the 'function' of reflexology, and then hypnobirthing. And as I write this, I realised something, by niching, back in 2013, and focusing on one area of my business – pregnancy - I began to miss the other aspects of what I did, namely working with people who were not pregnant. You see, what we bring to our business is the sum total of our life experiences, not just what we have learnt in such a short period of time. I was actually missing working with non- pregnant people.

I love working with a diverse range of individuals and I did not feel that this was quite happening for me.

Don't get me wrong, I loved working with pregnant people and their partners, but I did struggle with it just all being about birth and babies. Very often my way of thinking and approaching things was to look for how we could improve someone's thinking, and feelings overall, instead of just focusing on having a baby. Sound bizarre? Well it probably was, but that was how I felt at the time. Hypnobirthing never felt like enough, a few sessions of pregnancy reflexology never felt like enough, this was a lot about what had gone before for somebody, as well as the pregnancy journey they were facing now.

I work therapeutically with people, and if you think that is an icky word, then don't. I have been in therapy for most of my life, counselling when I was a student at university, psychotherapy when I was training to be a social worker, and then various forms of short-term counselling via the jobs I have done. Why? Because I truly believed that I could not get really good at what I do, and be supportive of others, without looking at my own life, my own experiences and making sense of them. What happened, though, left me in analytical overload.

I was a very open and expressive person, I always have been, and having someone else make sense of my experiences allowed me more things to hang my experiences onto. What I mean by that is that it triggered other things. I have a particular memory of a counsellor telling me that a lot of my issues, and work-related experiences were not work-related at all. They were actually down to the relationship I had with my mum.

Now this suggestion came way out of the blue, and I left that session feeling wrung out and extremely emotional. It was like the plaster had been pulled off, and the wound exposed, but it wasn't covered up before I left the session, and no real containment was offered. I remember that night lying in bed next to my husband sobbing, not really understanding what to make of it all. The reason I had initiated counselling in the first place was to deal with work-related issues with my then manager!

It was all such a confusing time, I was working on analysing my life, whilst doing a part-time job where I analysed peoples' behaviour to work out how they could best be supported. It was exhausting! When you deal with people who are vulnerable and in need every day, you give something of yourself, and some days you don't have much to give. That is so hard, especially when you are then trying to work out where all the other life experiences fit in too!

So why am I telling you this in amongst my website story? Well, the thing is, a lot of what

I was trying to do was stagnating because of my canny ability to analyse everything, and measure things often in light of what might go wrong. I was extremely good at taking action and 'doing', but my doing often slowed down after bursts of activity when that piece of action was completed. The websites were a prime example, they were something I could really get my teeth into, but they weren't going to bring me in a huge amount of income. I needed to get some other marketing strategies going, and that is where I very often got stuck.

At this time, as a successful pregnancy reflexologist and hypnobirthing teacher, with a steady stream of clients, what did I decide to do? Train to be a hypnotherapist!

Madness, I hear you think, here am I preaching about your ability not being defined by the amount of qualifications which you have, but I was doing just that, adding to my list of qualifications! What I know now, however, is that this was the qualification which was going to be defining in my list of qualifications. This was not because it made me 'better' or 'more qualified' to work with clients, it was because it gave me a firm grasp on how I was, and wanted, to live my own life.

I'm a bit reactionary when it comes to choosing courses. When people ask me about why and how I went about deciding to be a reflexologist, and how I chose a course, I have to be honest with them, I don't have much of a clue! All I really remember was that I had experiencing reflexology in my 20s, and then after I had my first son, was looking at ways which I could move away from the social work profession which, even at this time was draining me.

I didn't want to be away from my boy, I loved spending time with him, but I equally didn't want to not work, I needed to work for financial reasons but also for my sense of identity, for being me. At the time that sounded really selfish to me, I wanted to 'be myself' when I had just become a mum, but I recognise now that this was so important for me to have the energy and focus to be the mum I wanted to be. Doing my reflexology training was an additional drain on my time, but it gave me hope that work was not all about 9-5. The hypnobirthing training, as I have talked about earlier in this book, dovetailed neatly into what I was already doing, working with pregnancy reflexology clients. It allowed me to expand more offering, and in effect, increase my income. Honestly though, it also increased my outgoings, two websites, two different avenues of work, more resources and also more evenings and weekend work to fit in with the availability of pregnant couples.

It required dedication and commitment to even get the courses off the ground, due to gaps in the training, and from my point of view I was not going to do anything until I felt 100% happy with what I was teaching. The teaching also required ongoing learning given that the birth world was and is a fast-paced environment, ever changing and evolving, and to communicate and guide couples using the correct information, I was never standing still. My final big course choice, my hypnotherapy training, was again something I decided to do to give me a more in depth understanding of hypnosis and how the mind worked so I could better support my clients. I had long felt, from day one, that having a 'lovely hypnobirth' was not a qualification for being an amazing hypnobirthing teacher. Don't get me wrong, we all bring our own life experiences into our work, it certainly shapes why we do what we do, but I also didn't believe that this was a pre-requisite. I recognised that I was being a bit triggered here.

My first birth had been amazing, no hypnobirthing involved, just a fab midwife who really supported my husband to support me. My second birth, not so much, and it was only years later, after working with numerous hypnobirthing, and hypnotherapy clients that I realised I had experienced birth trauma during this birth, a very challenging realisation! I had a situation which you could describe as a 'how not to birth' scenario, an unsupportive midwife who just wanted me to do as I was told (people who know me know that I am not good at being told and will do the opposite)! The environment was not conducive to a calm peaceful, undisturbed birth, people coming in and out and the midwife constantly asking questions, and then the battle not to give birth flat on my back.

I was saddened by my experience, so glad it wasn't my first birth - which was amazing - and used it often in my courses to illustrate how you should not be treated. So, when I rocked up at my hypnobirthing training a few years later, all these calm, serene mamas (and can I just put on record that I hate the word 'mama', sorry if it offends but it makes me shiver every time I read it) I felt really inadequate because I hadn't done the 'hypnobirthing' thing!

What I realise now is that it didn't matter.

I didn't need to have had a hypnobirth. What we needed to learn was how to support a diverse range of expectant couples, or single women, from a variety of different backgrounds. This was my absolute strength, having been able, from my social work days, to approach the most extreme of situations and deal with the unexpected. This was my forte, just as supporting couples to have a home birth or understand the intricacies of birth were the forte of other hypnobirthing teachers.

The problem was, we all came out of that six-day training with a carbon copy course, and with the same 'cookie cutter' approach. Even now I read in group threads that this course needs to be taught in the way it has been trained in order to get the best results. Why was always my question, because everyone is at different points in their experience, their learning and understanding.

My skill, I believe, is to bring it all together, to meet the couple or couples where they are at and teach them what they need to know, dispelling the myths and building their confidence as they go. The one-size-fits-all approach was never my bag, never more of a challenge when teaching the expectant single parent. There is no way I could teach that carbon print of a course to her, devaluing her choices not to have a birth partner with her, which was the case in some situations.

So, when I dived into my hypnotherapy training, I kinda didn't really know, yet again, how I chose the course. Madness? Yes probably.

I went largely on location, I didn't want to go to London, I wanted to be able to come home in the evenings as it was a weekend course and that narrowed my options down quite a bit. I didn't have much criteria for the course, other than wanting to work with clients in a more diverse way. This was something I was already doing of my own volition, and I knew it was the right way forward for me.

I am a true believer that everything happens for a reason, and the courses I have chosen and worked through have certainly been no exception. Whilst I could have selected any course which would teach hypnotherapy, there are, like any subject, diverse methods, theories and principles underpinning the teaching. I decided, unwittingly, the course which was perfect for me at the time. So, when I rocked up on my first weekend, we were told our hypnotherapy was all about understanding how the brain worked, how to harness the power of the mind, understand it and apply it to everyday life to help us, and essentially our clients, to move forward. What they said made so much sense, I understood massively how powerful that could be and what I loved the most was there was no analysis! No working out why someone behaves the way they do and then trying to find a way forward. This was all about understanding that looking back was not as important as looking forward and making small positive steps in the right direction. I had no idea at the time how relevant this was going to be for me in my everyday life.

So, for a year I immersed myself in my course. I learned all about solution- focused hypnotherapy and positive moves forward. I gained a clear understanding that negative thoughts are the most powerful inhibitor to us progressing in our everyday lives and they contribute to our anger, anxiety and depression, which is so rife in our society.

The first person I had to apply it to was

myself, as I was one heck of a Negative Nancy. I measured all things in the light of what might go wrong, rather than what might go right. Despite all my teaching, studying and reading about the importance of a positive mindset, the practicalities weren't congruent with how I felt. Regardless of having an awesome website, gorgeous branding and fabulous coaching, I still wasn't being honest with myself about what I really wanted to do and achieve.

At the time of studying for this diploma, I was trying to leave my part-time job. This was relevant as fear was holding me back massively and I was so scared of what the future may hold if I took the plunge and became full time self-employed. So I just held on, feeling safe, believing that my business could fund its growth and my investments. But in reality it never really became self-sustaining. This was a scary time for me personally and professionally, but I truly believe that harnessing the small steps, and engaging in the amazing stuff which could happen (rather than all the stuff which might go wrong) helped me masses to take that brave step, way out of my comfort zone.

My learning on this course also supported me to help my children negotiate some tricky times too. My oldest was having a tough time with children at school, where he was learning that children were not nice all the time. This was leading to some tough lessons where he was finding out how to handle situations which previously had not been presented.

In such situations it is so easy to react in an angry way, storm up to school and demand that everything is sorted out. But how would that help him in the long run? Our approach was to take a step back, recognise the anger and then work out how to empower him to respond in a positive, confidence-building way.

How, I hear you ask, is this relevant to my therapy practice? Well, because, as you already know, our personal and professional lives are not mutually exclusive. What goes on in one directly affects the other and this was an opportunity to work through what I had learnt in 'real life' so to speak and enable my son to take a positive, forward-looking approach rather than feeling overwhelmed, negative and anticipating all the bad stuff which may, or may not happen.

I loved this year of study because, believe it or not, despite the frantic busyness of it all, it enabled me to see a positive way forward. A way which didn't make me feel bogged down in all the negative stuff or take up my headspace and drown me in overwhelm.

Myself and the other people I met on the course always said that whatever kind of month we'd had, we would walk into that training room and switch our mindset to positive and forward-looking, without really trying.

When you practice these principles in everyday life, you find that they really do work!

This training smoothed the way for me to leave my final paid, guaranteed source of income mid-way through the course. It felt massively empowering as well as positively petrifying.

It was a bit like being cut loose from chains which had held me for so many years, and for a good few months I wasn't too sure what to do with my newfound freedom.

I really struggled to get structure into my day unless it was booked up with clients, Again I was floundering with the plethora of learnings about what marketing I needed to do to make my business work, grow, thrive and prosper. I will be honest, the first two to three months without that regular income were really scary, and being in that place of fear was reflected back at me by the small income I brought in. I had, at this point, taken the step into becoming a limited company as I wanted to identify myself as a business owner in my own right, and at that time felt that becoming limited was the best way of going about this.

Would I have done this again if I had my time over? I am not sure.

What it did was help me secure the services of an awesome accountant and made me accountable for recording my income and expenditure on a monthly basis, rather than scrabbling around with receipts at the end of the year. Why is this important?

Well it helped me to know how on track I was with my expenditure, what my monthly earnings were and how I was gradually improving those earning month by month rather than flying by the seat of my pants and not knowing what was happening with my finances.

Don't get me wrong, I still battle with my conscience at the end of the month to get these completed and over to my bookkeeper. But to stay motivated, I reward myself when I have completed them and I'm always relieved when they're done. I find that whatever my perception of the month, I always seem to have brought in more than I thought I did - always a bonus!

Now, seeing as we have touched on money, and income, I am going to dive into this aspect of my business as it evolved. As I have mentioned, during the early days of running my business, my income was pretty spasmodic to say the least. Some weeks I would have no clients, other weeks I may have two or three. I look back now and realise that this was all I could have realistically managed, with all the other things going on in my life; namely two lively young boys who zapped every single ounce of my energy, and so they should! In the early days I priced my services to match the competition in my area.

But, I am going to be honest with you, I have had an issue with charging for my services for a long time. I worry about other people's affordability of my services and whether I am 'worth' what they are paying me. This had absolutely nothing to do with them and everything to do with my self-belief and confidence. What I know now, the financial affairs of a person buying my services or treatments has absolutely nothing to do with me. It's none of my business and it isn't up to me to question their choices, just as I would never expect anybody to question mine!

I received lots of support with my concept of money and charging, and lots of rational perspectives from marketing coaches. I sat down and literally worked through these steps, justifying how I could charge more, and what difference it would make to my income and how many hours I would have to work. The trouble was, whilst these structures and ways of positioning my business were immensely appealing, it did not do anything for my ability to truly believe in my self-worth, and so charging was still a big issue for me.

I look back now and know that this was part of my journey, and I do not beat myself up for this thinking. Part of the learning which they do not teach you on courses, is how to feel comfortable with charging, and valuing your services.

I cannot say this enough, looking at others in your local area or who do the same as you online, does not help. This only leads you to judge others' charging structures and their abilities. Do we all look the same, behave the same, act the same, do we all have exactly the same life experiences? The answer is a resounding NO and therefore who people are attracted to in our therapy industry are going to be wide and varied.

I was actually very accepting of some people who came and saw me for a treatment and did not come back, or who made an appointment and cancelled without reason. I never took offence, because everyone has a choice, and it was never a reflection of my success or failure as a therapist.

Likewise, the people who came to me for treatments and then referred others to me, were a natural evolution of the rapport and resonance I had built up with them. This made my work infinitely more enjoyable.

They were the clients I loved to treat, and really looked forward to seeing. Because it wasn't just a reflexology treatment, a hypnotherapy session, a hypnobirthing session. It was a dialogue which involved plenty of flowing positive communication and left both therapy-giver and therapy- receiver in a really good place. That is why our communication skills and building rapport is so vital. That is why it's about so much more than pricing. When people have that experience with you, the charging and money become secondary, and the regular bookings are just a natural evolution of the therapy relationship.

So, my biggest message here is, as someone who focused on the money and beat herself up for not charging enough, or not being able to truly charge what she felt she was worth, don't focus on the money!

Seriously, the money comes when the enjoyment and fun is there, when you look forward to a day of work and the clients you are going to see. Being aware of your finances and income and keeping track of it is one thing but getting hung up and panicky about where the clients are coming from is another.

I am going to be honest with you, I have never truly advertised my hypnobirthing, or put any true effort into marketing. What I did was just enjoy and value my teaching, and it all evolved from there. The best example of that was when I ran my first free 'taster' session. A number of people booked to attend, and I thought I would get one or two bookings from it. To my surprise, three quarters of the attendees signed up to attend a paid course, the majority of whom I had never met before! This led to a busy summer, and a lesson (make sure you set work/life boundaries, so you are not bending over backwards to accommodate everyone else).

The biggest challenge with hypnobirthing is the time constraints you have to teach your couples within - they will have their baby eventually! This would often set me off into panic mode and I'd find myself trying to accommodate everyone, at a date to suit them, which meant I worked every evening and weekend during the month of August, even the night before we went on holiday. I was knackered! Hand on heart, I am not sure whether my clients got the best of me because I was not giving myself space or any opportunity to rest and replenish between the sessions. The feedback was positive, though, it was just me who felt like a wrung-out dishcloth!

I kept promising myself that things would

improve, and I would stop worrying at the beginning of the month whether I would have enough money at the end to pay all my business expenses and household bills. This became more prevalent when I left my guaranteed position with the charity, and the business was totally reliant on what I put into it, and (pretty much, I believed at the time) how hard I worked!

When I look back now, I realised the pressure I was piling on myself was preventing me from actually growing my business and providing me with a consistent level of income. My head was too preoccupied with 'paid' employment and making a certain amount of money every month to pay the bills.

When I looked at my turnover (because I updated my accounts monthly, I had a good handle on my numbers) I realised that it always evened up. Even during the quieter months, I still managed to make up any shortfall the following month.

I still did have the 3am panics about where

the bookings were going to come from though, but they always came. Ironically, they would appear when I had a few days off and most often after a two-week holiday when I was refreshed and recharged. In 11 years, my client bookings have never come from advertising my treatments or classes, or from direct marketing, or writing advertorials in local magazines.

Even social media never drew paying clients to me. When I got around to posting, my engagement came from people who enjoyed connecting with me and reading about the positive responses I'd received from my clients.

Early on in my quest to market and grow my business, back in 2013, I was introduced to the concept of 'trading time for money'. At that time, I was in this category because I charged an hourly rate and people paid directly after their session with me. This meant I didn't have to invoice and so my cash flow was usually pretty stable. However, this 'time for money' was identified as a drain on time, resources, and energy, as well as limiting potential earnings and business growth.

At the time I was willing and receptive to every little nugget of information, and I took it on board fully. I wanted to grow my business, and this meant making more money, right? It all made sense. I worked alone, and therefore, I could only work so many hours and charge so much, couldn't I?

Herein lies the idea of 'passive income', something which was to play on me (and haunt me) henceforth, up until very recently.

Passive income can be defined as follows: you develop a product or service which does not require 'you' to be in it. You can record or develop something which people can buy, without your involvement. At the time it felt like the holy grail for therapists like me, making money while you slept? That sounded awesome and would grow my income at the same time.

My first attempt at this passive income stuff was a pregnancy relaxation recording. I was not a hypnobirthing teacher at this time and wasn't confident enough to think I could make my own recording. I was still stuck in the thinking that I needed to be a 'qualified' hypnotherapist to record something like this, and this was also the message I received from the marketing and business-growing groups I was in. So, I paid for another hypnotherapist to record this CD for me – yes, another investment.

In all honesty, I did exactly what I did with every other promotional tool to date. I created the product, put it on my website and didn't say anything about it! Hand on heart I paid £150 for this recording and to this day I have only ever sold two!

All these were my attempts to make more money, and grow my income in a 'passive' way, but I have come to hate the word 'passive' as it is sooo misleading. Seriously, when you create something which you want to exchange with people for money, you still have to be involved in its promotion; you still have to put it out there! I kinda did and hung it out there waiting for the magic to happen. And it never did, surprisingly enough, because

I was not talking about it, nor was I really understanding what it was for. I was just doing something someone else had told me to do because I desperately wanted to grow my business and make more money for me and my family.

This is a great example of why I struggle with formulas and 'how-tos'. They work for some people, but for a therapist who is used to being able to see different people every day of the week and respond to their needs, their emotions, in that moment, I really really struggled with the 'not being there' part of a 'passive' package.

This experience was the first step of my journey as I tried to create the 'online' income everyone was talking about. I was actually becoming pretty obsessed with not wanting to 'trade time for money' as I was continually being advised against it.

I love what I do, and this was the biggest obstacle to creating passive income. I am passionate about connecting with clients, and watching their transformation. Whilst I understood I could do this online, however, I could not get my head around how the whole thing would work. I understand now that this is because it wasn't right for me at that time. I was pushing something which did not resonate with me. I was creating products which I thought my clients would want, like my pregnancy relaxation recording, and not the things I loved. This is a subtle, but important, distinction and one which, in all honesty, I have only just recently learnt. Every time I wrote down what I could do for my clients, and the kind of problems I could solve, I was always thinking about them – and quite rightly so. My business was to support and help my clients in their everyday lives. However, it still needed to be about me, why I do what I do, and why I love it.

It is only now, after the past four years of immersing (and I mean immersing) myself in so much coaching and webinars and writing down my a-ha moments, that I have come to realise I didn't love anything I'd created.

One of the first online products I created was

a masterclass in transforming your sleep patterns, aptly named the 'Get Better Sleep' programme. Sleep, I identified, was a big problem for my clients, and so I created this programme to offer a solution. However, if I am really honest, I didn't feel excited about this programme or its content at all. I loved recording it, and I love sharing knowledge and information, but my launch did not spark peoples' interest, even though I thought and believed, it would! One person bought the programme, and although it was an evergreen programme that I could roll out time and time again, I didn't feel passionate enough about it to do so.

The story I told myself was that people didn't want to buy it because it wasn't meeting their needs. The reality was, I did not truly love it, and I just did not connect with the passion and desire for it to really gain momentum. I did not want to involve myself in dealing with peoples' sleep habits in this way.

It is always part of what I do, as so many people do have sleep issues, but it is not the sole-defining factor in my work. This felt compartmentalised, like I was doing something for the sake of it, and as a result it really didn't have the capacity to fly.

So I picked myself up and moved forward. I continued to look, and explore things on the basis of what my clients wanted, what I could provide (which would make me 'successful') and therefore earn myself a decent income and a thriving business.

What I failed to notice, however, at this time, was that my business was already thriving. I had a regular stream of old and new clients who I loved supporting. I thoroughly enjoyed helping them to transform their lives. This part of my business was in full, natural flow, and fit in with my everyday life. I worked when the boys were at school, and I was able to pick them up in the evening, do the 'mum thing' and then maybe work the occasional evening. I had truly achieved what I desired for so long, a balance between my home and work life. Did I recognise and celebrate that? Did I heck!

Oh no, my sole focus was now on establishing

a growing business online so I could make my fortune, just like all those gurus who claimed they'd turned their lives around and now make a million pounds a minute from the comfort of their yacht! Don't get me wrong, I had absolutely no aspiration to buy a yacht, nor was I seduced by millions. I just wanted to truly understand what it meant to 'transform' your life whilst working online, whilst still being able to really support your clients the way you wanted to. I didn't get it.

So off I went, back to the drawing board with the online stuff, whilst still pondering about who I wanted my ideal client to be.

Okay, 'ideal client', let's deal with that one first, shall we?

On reflection, pinpointing the ins and outs of my ideal client was one of the most difficult things I had to work through when attempting to grow my business. Yes, in the early days I had created my niche of pregnant women who were stressed out and needed support during their pregnancy, and this led me to train and teach hypnobirthing.

I was still, however, attracting a lot of women who were trying to get pregnant too, and need my therapy support. This resulted in a tug – what did I actually want to focus on, could I focus on both, should I focus on one, how would it all hang together if I had such a limited amount of time?

I became very hit and miss with my marketing. One minute I was creating this amazing profile of this stressed-out pregnant woman, where she lived, what she did, and where she holidayed. I was a great storyteller! Then I was looking at a profile of someone trying to get pregnant, but was it first or second time, should I focus even deeper?

If I am really honest I never really felt comfortable with either profile. But, again, I was following the guidance of other successful people who kept telling me this was the 'right' way to do things. I believe now, that I needed to do this, and I fully appreciated the support I received and the learning and understanding I gained along the way.

If I hadn't immersed myself in this learning

and understanding, I would still be that 'generic' therapist trying to appeal to everyone, and in the process not distinguishing herself from the crowds of other reflexologists out there.

However, what I know now is that I niched myself so specifically, I stopped myself evolving as fully as I truly wanted to. I still attracted 'other' client groups, stressed-out, worn-out mums, and husbands of these mums who worked in the corporate world. These clients held true meaning for me, as I knew I could truly transform their everyday lives with my reflexology.

My hypnotherapy training and expertise brought me back into that field of being able to support a variety of people, and I found I attracted a large amount of people with anxiety.

Hear that word 'attract'. I did not identify these people using an ideal client 'avatar'. Instead, I started to talk about who I helped and could help, and people chose me based on this information. My thinking had evolved significantly and I now strongly believed two things.

1. That people needed as much information as possible to be able to make a choice. This did not mean I had to add reams of information to my website, it was more about interactions in a variety of different ways, including the evolving social media, which I will come back to in a moment.

2. The second was, and still is, rapport. One of the most significant things I have learnt over the years is that people who are looking for support need to feel a connection with you, and feel comfortable with you.

Often it has taken a huge amount of courage and faith to address the issues which they feel would benefit from therapy, be it reflexology or hypnotherapy, and it can be an effort just to cross the threshold of my treatment room. The most significant conversation I remember was with a mum of a teenage daughter last year.

She contacted me after following my Facebook page and reading my posts (which were mainly about the challenges I faced as a mum and bringing up my two boys). She told me about her daughter's panic attacks, and explained that she had seen a variety of therapists but her daughter found it hard to connect with them. Her mum was, understandably, very worried about her daughter and she explained that while these well-meaning individuals kept asking her how she 'felt', her daughter didn't really know. She had reached the point where she dreaded the question being asked in the end, knowing that she was going to have to give some kind of answer.

I talked to this mum and explained that if I was going to be able to help at all, both she and her daughter would have to feel comfortable with me – this was the single most important thing. To establish this connection, I invited them to meet me.

My 'type' of therapy, I felt, may be the best option for this young girl because we don't spend all our time talking about 'feelings' nor do we dwell on what has happened in the past. But unless she felt comfortable with me, nothing positive would be achieved in the long-term to move her forward. I truly did not want to be another therapist in her long list of therapists as I believed it would do more harm than good.

So from this point spins the debate about the free 'initial consultation' which often has people divided, especially when the 'trading time for money' debate rears its head.

I have been pulled in both directions over this, but have landed in the camp of offering this time for people to meet me and talk through where they are at and what they want to achieve. I want people to feel confident that they are committing to something which they think can help them, and understand how it will, before actually committing to it. And in the process, it's an opportunity to meet me, a normal person (or relatively normal) with a normal everyday life, facing similar challenges and overcoming them day by day. I don't wear a uniform, even for my reflexology treatments, I don't have a clipboard. Yes, I fill in a consultation form but that's an aide memoire for myself to ensure I provide the best possible support.

My aim has evolved over time into taking steps to break down the barriers of what 'therapy' means. To me, it means a true positive, open communicative relationship between client and therapist, where talking in a comfortable, safe environment is the absolute priority. One of my absolute favourite phrases is this 'I hold space for you until you feel able to hold it yourself' and this has stood firm for me throughout my years working, and evolving in this field.

So what about this 'social media stuff'?

When I started out as a therapist, 11 years ago, we were still on dial-up internet! The worldwide web was growing all the time, but social media was a relatively new concept. My first taste of finding, building and resuming connections was 'Friends Reunited'. It was a platform which allowed you to find out what your school pals had been up to since leaving, and was generally a nosy around into other people lives, or more to the point, what other people wanted to share! It took me a long time to get into this world of social media, and if I am really honest I am not sure I want to be as involved as I am. It has, however, worked wonders for my ability to reach out and support people, both directly and indirectly.

Don't get me wrong, I have had a love/hate relationship with this new-fangled arena of communicating for years and years. Most often it's when I'm sitting, poised to post, and I have no idea what to write. My relationship with the beast is a book in itself, and it is one I have had to tame and make my own as I have evolved. I have spent hours watching tutorials, getting help with ads, boosting posts, reading about strategy, and watching masterclasses, yet still my relationship with it all was pretty hit and miss.

What I realise now is that I was trying too hard to make it fit a perfect model, plus I was spending far too much time watching what other people were doing, and comparing it to my own efforts. I believe that when we indulge in comparison-itis, social media becomes a more challenging area to overcome. At least when you are researching websites you have to consciously Google people and businesses, and then click your way around their site. But with social media you can be merrily browsing away, and something can pop up unexpectedly on your newsfeed which triggers all those feelings of:

- Ooh no I'm not doing that!

- Should I be doing that?

- They've got loads of interaction from that post.

- Will my business fail if I don't keep posting?

I will give you an example - gift vouchers for therapies, which obviously become very significant around Christmas time. I hear other therapists (and here comes the comparison-itis again) raving about how they sell loads of vouchers and they're then busy right through January fulfilling those orders.

Green-eyed monster here? Well I used to be, as apart from the odd purchase, gift vouchers were never really my 'thing'. I am totally not sure why. I often thought it was because I didn't 'sell' them in the right way, maybe people didn't know about them. I mention them though, and last year I did a whole Facebook ad campaign about the vouchers without one iota of interest.

The lesson here for me, now that I have had time to reflect, is that I am trying too damn hard. Seriously, if people want vouchers, they will ask me. If I talk about them and they are keen, they will buy them.

I believe this comes down to different client groups again, and what different therapists offer. The people I attract are in it for the long-haul, they get that and are happy to invest in their own treatments. I don't really attract those who are interested in 'one-off' pamper treatments. If people come to me for one-off treatments, it's usually for a specific issue. Why? That's the way I roll.

Every single therapist attracts different client groups, and has positive and enduring relationships with them, and this may result in the purchase of gift vouchers. The best thing I ever did was to let go of the need to 'sell' these at this time of year, and, instead, get on with doing what I love - supporting the clients who still need me, even in December and particularly in December when the stress, and expectation of Christmas can become even more pronounced.

So where does this all leave me with the social media experience? Well, when I look back to previous years' posts, I realise how much I have evolved. Again, I used to plan and prepare posts in advance to make sure I had something flying out there on a pretty much daily basis. But what I found was that the posts of mine people engaged with were ones I had written off-the-cuff, in the leisure centre car park whilst my son was at swimming. It might be a post sparked off by another article which I found thought- provoking and wanted to share, or it may have been an experience with a client or my children or myself which led me to think about it more deeply, and realise it could be relevant to the wider community (my Facebook page).

I stopped trying to be specific and started to be me. If something got my goat, I talked about it, if I was proud of something, I mentioned it. I was surprised how many people read what I wrote, much of which had nothing to do with 'therapy' but everything to do with it in the same breath.

Why? Because everything I spoke about led my followers to get to know the real me, that I could be vulnerable, and scared and overwhelmed too, and I was not this professional sitting on a pedestal ready to tell you how to change your life for the better, or highlight everything which was wrong. I felt that the people who were reading my stuff derived value from it because they felt like we were connected, and shared similar experiences, and they were so grateful to discover they were not alone in their own battle.

I write about this like it was a natural evolution, but it wasn't. I had to spend time sitting with it, and writing about it, getting it wrong, crying at my desk and not having a clue what I was doing. Creating memes in Canva that meant nothing to me other than being a way of getting my message out there. It was therapy in itself and this was the part of the business which scared me the most. Until I could move through my stuff and overcome my fears and self-confidence issues, all these things would be triggered every time I tried to talk about my business through social media.

This is why, I believe, as I moved through that healing journey, received the support of my EFT practitioner and continued to receive the support of a variety of different coaches, the way I was able to show up on my page evolved to where I am today - honest, authentic and just a little bit quirky.

So, as my social media has evolved along with me, so has my website. After leaving my 'paid' job and sinking into my business full- time, I gradually began to look at different ways I could invest time and effort into my business to showcase my expertise. As I talked about earlier, I had my branding created, and it reflected what I loved, not what I believed others wanted to see and how they wanted to see it. I loved it, and others did too.

By this point, I (eventually) decided that the time had come to merge my two Facebook pages - Marlow Reflexology and Blissful Birthing - because having two pages, and two websites was frankly doing my head in.

What I have learnt over the years is that if we spread our focus then we dilute our effort, and to be honest, everything else becomes diluted.

I used to get really frustrated with myself when nothing ever got finished on either website. I was always playing catch up and I never really loved what I had done because I didn't have the time or the energy to sit with my copy on both sites. Of course, it didn't help that I was my own worst critic too and I just felt split down the middle. Then, a lovely coaching lady I was speaking to said something which really resonated with me.

She told me that I was thinking and acting like by businesses were separate, and therefore it was a struggle to make things come together in the right way for me, given that I was giving energy to two different things.

It was a bit like going back to a part-time job again, having two things to juggle, grow and focus on. I took her reflections and pondered on them, and realised that she was totally right. I was still trying too hard to be all things to all people, and in the process, despite 'niching', I had expanded in two different areas and in turn, my message as to how I could help and support people and transform their lives had become blurred.

This realisation made me even more determined to create the 'Clare Cogan' brand, reflecting who I was not just what I could do. If I was rooted so firmly in belief that people buy people, then those interested in working with me needed to really see the person behind the skillset.

So, how did I do this? Well firstly I bought a new domain name, clarecogan.com. It felt really egotistical to base my business on me, a bit 'egocentric' but I realised over time that it wasn't that at all. I was, in effect, developing an opportunity for people to learn all about me, and what better name than mine? Over the years I had toyed with, asked opinions on, and generally got stuck with trying to come up with the 'perfect' business name - which I now know doesn't exist!

What you actually need to find is something which resonates, a name which resonates and reflects what you do and how you want to be seen out there in a busy marketplace. I needed to be me, and identify more with myself more than just 'I am a hypnotherapist' or 'I am a reflexologist'. Niching into the pregnancy arena and developing my 'ideal client' persona had sort of helped, but it wasn't until I really focused in on the 'Clare Cogan' brand that things started to make sense to me.

So, with a new domain name, comes a new website, and an opportunity to bring everything together under one umbrella. I was ridiculously excited and looked for someone who could build this site for me. I don't know whether it was my journey with websites, or because it was so personal, but the person I chose (the lovely guy who I had worked with twice before was no longer building websites) just could not grasp what I wanted. It wasn't her fault, I was literally moving so quickly from what I wanted to focus on and how I wanted it to look, that I couldn't get a grip on it myself, let alone communicate it to someone else!

Eventually we parted company, on good terms, and I learnt a huge lesson. Don't be afraid to admit when something isn't right, if it doesn't feel right then it is not right. Don't feel beholden because you have paid someone some money. If the relationship and what is being produced just doesn't work for you then take that decision. We are all the CEOs of our businesses, we need to make major decisions sometimes about when to stop a project, move in a different direction and even lose money when we feel it isn't right for us anymore. This website development just wasn't working for me, and this dragged me into a place of real panic. If I couldn't find someone who could help me with my website, how the heck was I going to do it?

One of my personality traits is that I like to understand things. I enjoy learning and educating myself. It is why, over the most recent years, I have not felt the need to do formal CPD courses, just pick up educational elements along the way, which most of the time have been business focused. So I have done blogging workshops, used other peoples' tutorials to learn how to use YouTube and other techie stuff, and I decided that the technology of a website was going to be no exception.

A lovely lady with whom I had previously worked, had developed a 'build your own website' course and I used her step-by-step process to do just that! Having my branding done for me helped masses, with the fonts, colours and styles already combined to something which was eye-catching and stunning, I just needed to create the structure and bring it all together with the copy. I was going great guns until I got to the copy and layout of the site, and I realised that I was still struggling with what I really did.

It was so hard not to fall into that default setting of 'I'm a reflexologist' or 'I am a hypnobirthing teacher' and each time I said it I used to cringe a little bit as I knew that was not truly who, or what I was. I could write copy. I loved writing (can you tell!) but I couldn't sew everything together in the way that I felt comfortable. So I left it, sort of hanging, with a bit of stuff on it, but not much. I just wasn't quite ready to evolve into 'clarecogan.com'.

So what happened once the website was up and running? It wasn't much different to what I had been doing before, seeing reflexology and hypnotherapy clients, running hypnobirthing courses, loving meeting new people and seeing the positive outcomes from their treatments.

I was still doing the dreaded 'trading time for money' but I could not see a way out of that, I was a therapist, right?

Therapists see clients and get paid for it, all

my other therapy friends around me worked in this way, and some were much busier than me - which I tried hard not to get distracted by, even after 11 years of running my practice.

A long time ago I decided I did not want to be one of those therapists who worked every hour of every day, seven days per week. I was clear with myself, after my early experiences of juggling a job, a business and a family that this was not the way to go.

The whole point of realising my passions and working in my own business was so that I did not have to compromise time with my boys, and to do the 'mum' thing which always was my priority. So when my boys were sick I did not worry about having to take a day off work and explain it to someone else. When I needed to go to a school assembly I could, and if I had to work the odd evening or weekend, it was always around my boys' activities, so I could be on hand to drop them off and pick them up.

These were my 'rules' to ensure that I did not cripple myself with 'mum guilt' at every available opportunity. I look at my boys, who are now 12 and 9 and I realise that although they will always be my boys, there isn't that much time left for them to 'need' me in their lives. Right now, I love to see them grow and flourish, try new things and have fun in their lives, but their dependency on me is reducing. But while my eldest son loves his physical independence I do find he needs me more emotionally now, and I love the fact that I am able to be there for him whenever he needs me.

But I can't say it's been easy growing my business and being mum too. There have been some pretty tough times, but I've always known there was something keeping me in my business, even in my darkest hours, when I've been crying on a call with my coaches or messaging my business friends and telling them I just couldn't do it anymore. I always knew I would sustain my business, but my crippling self-doubt and anxiety sometimes caught me completely unaware and floored me.

When you work in your own business you

really do have to have your 'why', your raison d'être. I always found this the hardest part to connect with, and sometimes avoided doing it when anybody asked me.

I've created vision boards, set intentions, and written goals, but not in any kind of strategic way, just in the way I am feeling in that moment. My 'why' has always been set in the foundation of being the mum I wanted to be, not like in the early days of being a social worker where I was compromising my emotional health and being present with my boys for a part-time flexible job which paid me a reasonable salary. No money can replace being emotionally energised and able to respond to whatever your children bring home from their school day.

I didn't want to be preoccupied with my 'work stuff' and wanted the 'bad day' mentality to be a thing of the past.

And then I knew that my 'why' was keeping me going. When I saw how my business could really help me personally as well as impact on the lives of others. Rather than reacting to everything, I was learning how to just do what I needed to, and more importantly, enjoy it. If nothing else, hypnotherapy taught me that how we respond and feel about a situation affects our thoughts, which then govern our emotions. The more I spent time doing what I wanted rather than what I felt I needed to do, the better I felt in myself and the more positive reactions I received from my clients.

I have many regular clients who have come to see me for years and I believe that this is down to two main things. One is I give people my time, and attention, I ask about them and their lives and show an interest in them. This is so necessary when building rapport. I also don't 'conveyor belt' clients. Some therapists I see are back-to-back all day, evenings and most weekends. They are exhausted, and it shows. This is born out of fear that they have no idea where the next client is coming from, and I totally relate to that.

But even when I was at my lowest points, when I was working, raising a young family and running a business and when I was grieving for my friend, the clients just kept coming. I don't know why, or how, I had no business strategy or marketing campaign, I just looked after myself and managed to conserve what energy I did have to see these valued clients and ensure a level of transformation in their lives. Most therapists will know that when we give a good treatment, we benefit too, the law of reciprocation comes into play here. However, if we are drained and exhausted it will show in our energy and I have learnt over the years to accept that when clients cancel, or I have a quieter week, it is because I need to rest and recuperate. I don't take it as a sign that there are no clients out there and they are never coming back, I see it as an opportunity to enjoy doing some other things that I don't usually have time for.

Now, I see a maximum of four clients per day, and that is enough for me. It provides me with the opportunity to nurture and support those who need it whilst maintaining my energy levels.

I have learnt these lessons about myself after years of self-doubt, anxiety and a complete lack of self-belief. What writing this book has reminded me of is how far I have come. Yes, I have taken others' advice and guidance, and I have made huge leaps along the way from their support. However, if my head hasn't been in the right place, if I haven't been 'feeling it' then I very often lapsed back into old behaviours and fears.

What I now understand is that others can tell you what to do and how, but they are not you, they do not know truly what it is like to be you, and they can only offer support from their standpoint. I thought I could build a thriving business from getting someone else to tell me how to do it, but all that did was get me more stuck.

One example of this was an online community I created. It was for mums who needed a bit of calm in their life and it was a monthly membership club with a small monthly payment. I loved the concept of bringing a community together to support each other with one common aim - to move away from the judgement and self-criticism which often surrounds us mums and support us with the dreaded 'mum guilt'. For a while I loved it, I enjoy connecting with people and lifting them up because building confidence in others is what I do (the tools being the reflexology, the hypnotherapy etc).

However, despite the positive responses I got from my small community, I could not feel my way into growing it.

I got 'stuck' with knowing what to say and when to say it. Everything felt hard and stunted, and I was very conscious that I needed to regularly and consistently provide something for people who were paying to hear from me and engage with our community. All this pointed towards the realisation that this was the wrong direction for me. The motivation to support these mums and build their confidence was still there, but the mechanism, I realise now, was all wrong.

What did I learn from this?

If you are creating something to fulfil a

demand, rather than because you love it, your heart won't be in it. I was pushing something out there I just did not feel aligned to and it showed. Now that was a huge dose of honest from me, and something I believe every therapist, and business owner can learn from.

Do not do something just because Joe Bloggs is doing it, because someone else tells you that this was the way they made their million. That is their journey, not yours.

As you know, I have been on my therapist path for 11 years now and when I started out, I had no clue it would get me to the point I am at now. On the day I qualified all I envisaged was running a business and seeing regular clients at set times which slotted around my life and enabled me to give up other paid employment.

What I did not anticipate was all the rocks in the road, the challenges and the pitfalls which came from me not having the confidence to shine and fearing the unknown.

So my evolution as a therapist, a business

owner and a creator of online courses (sort of) was about to take another very unexpected turn.

Over the years as a therapist I had tried and tested a whole range of the creams I used on clients' feet. Firstly, I chose the cream which was recommended by my pregnancy reflexology trainer. I had this desire to use a cream with essential oils because I knew they would aid my clients' relaxation during the treatments. I had been introduced to essential oils during my first pregnancy, when my midwife suggested a combination of tea tree and lavender in the bath to aid healing.

I found a lovely aromatherapist and reflexologist who created products for exactly the use I had been looking for, and happily used her products for a number of years. During that time, I was continually looking out for something which would enable me to actually personalise the products I was using in my treatments. One size does not fit all, as far as I'm concerned, and when I sensed my clients needed something unique, I knew essential oils could create a more bespoke solution.

I did not want to train in aromatherapy massage, I have hypermobility which means my joints are uber-flexible and ache more easily, especially when applying consistent amounts of pressure. I was overjoyed when I found a training course 'aromatherapy for the feet' which trained us in using and blending key oils for use with clients.

It was a one-day course but very informative. However, my heart sank at the end of the day when we were told the course did not cover us for working with pregnant women. At this time, pregnant women were my main clients. So what could I do?

My desire to work with essential oils has been around for ages, but I had no idea how to tap into it. I did not just want them to smell nice when they went on the feet, I wanted them to actually do what they said they were meant to do. Yes, I was often directed to essential oil suppliers, but when you are faced with an alphabetical list of one hundred and one essential oils and you have an aromatherapy az next to you, it is difficult to know where to start.

So I didn't.

Now this part of my story has two parts - the introduction above was the context of my story. The next part may not seem entirely relevant but bear with me, it will make sense as you read on.

Whilst running my therapy business over the years I have met and networked with a lot of people. In the early days this was the best possible way to make my business more visible, to talk about it, and explain the benefits of the therapies I offered.

I never attended networking meetings with the anticipation of 'getting' clients, I went because I enjoyed meeting new people and sharing experiences of running a business.

I did go to a 'paid for' networking event once and felt very stilted. Why? There was a structure, everyone had to do things in a certain order and we were expected to identify people we could refer on to others. Now that is totally not the way I work.

I recommend other businesses without hesitation, IF I have connected with them in an authentic, natural way, and often when I have used their services.

I will not send my clients off to use the services of someone else on the basis of an 'elevator pitch'. I also believe that networking is reciprocal, so people coming with the hope of receiving lots of business without taking the time to really give back are going to be disappointed. So, my network of people I refer to is small, but I know that if I refer on to them, my client is going to get an exceptional service, and I maintain one of my business priorities - integrity.

I had to find my level with networking, and it took time, energy and commitment to properly get to know people and enjoy spending time with them, rather than thinking, here we go, another boring networking event. I don't believe they are a waste of time, but I do believe that the ones which only allow one of each 'type' of business, and which structure everything to the enth degree, lack the ability to have a free-flowing group who can express their personalities and warmth.

It was in the networking arena that I first came across what are called Multi-Level Marketing (MLM) or Network Marketing businesses. They kind of went over my head at first, they were just another business selling their products and I listened politely as they talked about their businesses. What I noticed over time, though, was that more people from the same businesses turned up, and they all seemed to be saying the same thing. The products, as they claimed, seemed to be amazing, but I wasn't actually sure what made the difference buying from one person as opposed to buying from another.

And then they upped the ante. These business members began approaching me and inviting me for a coffee so we could talk about me selling their products to my clients. As I outlined before, I have been on a journey with finding therapeutic creams and oils to use with my clients, and at that time I was still on said journey.

The thing is, I have this personality trait. Some might call it stubborn, others might say uncompromising. For me it is honed from a number of years running my own business and developing a tenacity from making my own decisions and having to own them. I did not want to use other peoples' products in my business, no matter how amazing they told me they were. I was not seduced by the amazing reviews and the refined, environmentally-friendly nature. This all sounded like a well-rehearsed sales pitch to me and I wasn't buying into it. And I wasn't stupid, either. I knew I was being hunted down as a 'prospect' to promote these products as part of my business, and why not? After all, I was an ideal client for these representatives.

Now don't get me wrong, I don't blame these people for doing what they felt was right in their own business, but I became very suspicious of anyone wanting me to try their products for the exact reason that I did not want to be sold to.

I hold my hands up, I held a very prejudiced attitude towards these kind of businesses, mainly from my experience with certain individuals, and the style of selling that went with it. I was very judgemental, and far too quick to form an opinion or make an assumption.

What I really disliked was the material incentives that were offered – the brand new cars, fancy 5* holidays and all the other luxurious trappings designed to push you to reach sales and recruitment targets month on month. But something kept chipping away at me, and I didn't really know what.

So, that's the background to the story which leads me up to this point, and by now I hope it will all make sense. I was checking my emails one afternoon and noticed one from a local therapist I had used for treatments on and off over the years. She was a well-respected therapist in her area and regularly held classes and workshops. She'd contacted me to let me know about some classes she was running which introduced essential oils into therapy practices, and how this could be done, even if you weren't a qualified aromatherapist.

I was floored. I had no idea that this was possible. Since day one it had been drummed into us that if we didn't have a qualification in a certain therapy, we couldn't use or practice it.

That was why I always felt so restricted with the creams and oils I used with my clients, because I was too scared to step out of the restrictions which my therapy and insurance placed on me.

The excitement was palpable, I had been looking for and asking about therapeutic grade essential oils for pretty much as long as I had been a therapist. Was this the answer?

I met with this lady one frantic morning in the middle of the summer holidays. I had no idea what to expect. I can't even remember much of the conversation, just that I wanted the oils to try. I bought my first kit, 10x 5ml bottles of the key oils for health and wellness. They arrived three days later, and two days after that I succumbed to my son's cold. I remember contacting my therapy friend to ask her for the best oil to use. She advised me to use peppermint, but to be cautious and if I were inhaling it, just to use one drop. I did as she instructed, and it nearly blew my head off! It eased my congestion and cleared my head and from that moment I loved essential oils.

It is really hard to describe the transformation I experienced from using the oils in my day-to-day life and with my children, and clients. Using them daily and wanting to share them with others meant I ran out of my 5ml bottles extremely quickly. But this was exactly as it should be. I couldn't believe I'd been missing out on these wonderful oils throughout my entire career as a therapist. If only I'd found out earlier that they did what they were supposed to do, both physically and emotionally, and they smelt gorgeous too.

The feedback I received about the oils was awesome. I began to hear how they had settled anxious tummies, managed moods and extreme stress, and had been hugely helpful with physical ailments too, such as colds, coughs and ear ache. People loved them because they felt that all-important change, and that's where the magic starts.

I was on a bit of an accelerated learning journey with these beautiful oils, but I got my head down like I always had in my business and got up to speed with what I needed to know. I am no expert, I never profess to be, I very often just picked out an oil I felt would help based on what someone was saying to me and then used it in their treatment, be it hypnotherapy or reflexology.

Hypnobirthing and pregnancy reflexology was a bit more challenging for me as we are so cautious when using anything on pregnant women. I then read a book called *The Essential Midwife* by Stephanie Fritz. Her anecdotes about how she had helped women during their pregnancies and in labour, and continued to do so, made me feel more and more comfortable about working in this area.

The thing is, when we break stuff down and look at where the caution has come from, it is very rarely based on logical (or sometimes even rational) evidence. I learnt this a lot when I taught hypnobirthing. When the same piece of research is given out time and time again as a rationale for some kind of action or intervention in birth, you look into that research and find a number of generalised anomalies which do not make it as strong, or as viable as first thought.

The importance of mentioning this is because Chinese whispers and subjective opinion can be very convincing, and not in a forward-looking, enlightening way. They can actually hold people back from discovering their true potential or finding solutions to long-held problems.

Often these views and opinions are based on fear. Fear of doing something differently, fear of getting it wrong, or fear of the implications. In my work as a hypnotherapist I see that fear is simply the brain's misinformed way of keeping us safe, of stopping us breaking through into new and positively beneficial experiences. When you logically look at whether it is safe to use one drop of lemon oil, for example, diluted heavily in a carrier oil to massage on the feet and relieve symptoms of pregnancy- related sickness, is this something which we need to fear, really and truly? When we think about the toxins we come into contact with every single day, is one drop of lemon oil going to harm us?

And this has been my biggest learning to date, from all my courses, all my qualifications, all my teaching. You have to find your own way, a way which works for you, and which you feel confident about. This is relevant in everyday life as well as the professional life as a therapist. If it doesn't feel right, then don't do it. I have only ever been unable to give reflexology to two people in my entire career, because I evaluate the circumstances, and make a decision based on an individual's situation.

I have met reflexologists who won't touch a woman's foot before 12 weeks. I will but I make sure I am comfortable with my client's history and background and the context of giving a treatment so that they are fully informed. I have also met a number of fertility therapists who won't treat during an IVF cycle, stress the importance of protocols which need to be followed (basically selling a training course).

I took this advice on board and one of my clients (who I had been seeing me for months) actually cried in my treatment room because I said I couldn't see her during her long-awaited cycle of IVF.

My first priority is to my clients, not the rules, and unless there is a clear medical contraindication, I will support my clients' physical and emotional wellbeing.

Now, it has taken me a number of years to profess this confidently, and out loud. I understand how, as a newly qualified therapist, I lacked confidence. I was let out into the big wide world to practice what I had learnt, having had the rules and regulations drummed into me. I felt too scared to even think about crossing those boundaries.

Now don't get me wrong here, I do understand we have to work within certain safety protocols, but what I quickly realised was that some of these safety rules were not really justifiable, or necessary, they just served to hold people back from truly being the therapists they want to be.

One of my most poignant moments of working outside the lines was when I developed a short course for doulas to introduce them to a range of basic reflexology techniques to use with their clients during their birth. I recognised that although I could attend births as a reflexologist, I was rarely practically able to do this. To date I have been present with two clients in early labour and had one client go into labour when I was working on her feet! My rationale was to introduce the calming nature of reflexology, and as an introduction I was supporting doulas to enhance the support they gave to women.

However, others did not share my viewpoint. There was a small cohort of reflexologists who (behind my back and never to my face) judged what I was intending to do. They felt it was 'risky', and the previous professional association I belonged to also discouraged me. They thought it would prevent people from finding 'properly trained' reflexologists.

Well, in my opinion, people were being exposed to inadequately trained reflexologists every day, people who attended a weekend course, usually beauty therapists, who went on to provide treatments. This introductory course was about sharing basic concepts, and the doulas knew it was simply to provide them with an additional skillset. So, I took myself through these challenges, and remained firm in my views. This is what made the difference between my business thriving and not thriving, I was willing to be me and not cower and question when I was told I couldn't do something. The stubborn streak in me would always question something if I was told I couldn't, sometimes to my detriment because I have been pulled down different paths which were not as successful as others. But with all of them, lessons were learned to allow me to reflect and do things differently next time and my integrity remained intact as I always kept my individual client at the centre of my approach. This is, I believe, what made me, and continues to make me a successful therapist.

So what has this got to do with my move into the world of essential oils, you might be wondering?

Well, as I started to use these oils in my treatments, people loved them, and wanted to buy them, and this is the one thing I have neglected to mention. doTERRA, the company who sources, produces and supplies the essential oils has chosen network marketing as the model to share the amazing therapeutic value of these oils. Not good! After years of side-stepping the attempts of others to 'recruit me' to sell whichever MLM it was, I had now joined a network marketing company!

This was, without doubt, a huge block for me. I knew that people where joining these organisations to make a living, and I commended people who did. But I did not like seeing people who spent their days posting on their personal timelines about how amazing their products were, and how everyone should try them, buy them or join their fast-growing team. I also did not appreciate being added to groups without my permission so I could 'learn more'. I was prejudiced, and judgmental, and I was looking for any excuse to ditch this terrible company!

But they weren't terrible, at all.

I questioned every aspect of their 'PR' looking for propaganda, salesy stuff, and most importantly 'pressure' to sell.

But there wasn't any.

My major concern was rooted in the values I had developed as a therapist over the years – of integrity and placing the client at the centre. This oily business was no exception, and I did question how people who had no concept of safety, cautions and contra-indications could go ahead and recommend products to others. This aspect of the business felt, at first, to be too salesy for me, but I had yet to experience the journey I would take a client on.

Now some people would say that it was easy for me, having a therapy business with clients I could 'sell to'. But in all honesty, pinky promise, I didn't 'try' to sell, the oils sold themselves!

The first time I did a Facebook live on my business page about how one of the oils had helped my youngest son settle at night and sleep well, someone went and bought the oils!

I was flummoxed. All I had done was share my own personal experience of our success. And then I realised something. People are always looking for solutions in their lives. Over the years I had built up credibility with my 'crowd', my 'audience', and my 'tribe'. I don't have a name for these lovely people in my world, I was just grateful they joined me and even listened to what I had to say!

I, over time, discovered the difference between how I had been 'sold to' all these years by MLMs and what was happening with me. It was first and foremost, an education, a journey, and it was for anyone who was interested in learning more.

This model absolutely suited me down to the ground. I was not expected to 'sell products', I was expected to 'share' them, with no money changing hands! Woohoo, I loved that,

I could support and educate people, and transform lives. Then it was totally up to them whether they made a purchase, no selling from me was required.

The further distinction I made was that I was providing products which enabled people to improve their lives from the inside out. They learned they could stabilise their mood, support their immune system, and deal with emotional issues rather than finding products which just addressed the looking good on the outside. The combination of inside and out was, and still is, immensely powerful.

However, on this journey of reflection, I also realised something else. How judgmental I had been of all those women who were involved in MLM businesses, and I felt quite ashamed of myself. I became very aware of the Facebook groups I belonged to, outwardly criticising and refusing to buy from any MLM, refusing to read posts or allowing them to comment on questions and queries, even if they could genuinely help.

Don't get me wrong, these products still held

absolutely no interest to me. I had made my choice, and my essential oils journey was one I had only just embarked on, and was immensely looking forward to, but I started to feel sorry for these other women.

After all, most of these groups were all about empowering, and nurturing women in business, but, it seemed, only certain women in business! Many times I have wanted to stop doing what I am doing within the business which is doTERRA Essential Oils, and feeling judged because I was part of an MLM. Comments like 'pyramid scheme', 'over-priced' and 'unethical company' are regular themes bandied around, mainly on social media.

To be honest though, I don't get involved in these discussion as I would just be wasting energy on trying to convince someone to engage in trying a product which they are determined not to like. What I did do was talk about them a lot on my Facebook business page.

All of a sudden, I had something I loved

which was tangible to talk about, that could truly help others, with or without me being present. Plus (and this is the best bit), I could support them on their journey, learn and understand more, and have fun doing it.

So my free Facebook group became my medium of communication, a place to offer support and guidance. I noticed the positive effects straightaway. People reached out and connected with me who never had before, many of whom weren't geographically close to me but that didn't matter.

Over the years I have discovered that people often shy away from 'therapy'. For whatever reason it was a word which did have negative connotations for some people, but oils seemed to bridge that gap and got people accessing support and guidance in a more acceptable way at the beginning of their journey.

I am a giver, and this works perfectly for me because I now had something to share. I could give these oils, and my time, to people.

In doing this, the strangest thing happened. My income flowed effortlessly, without me having to 'work' at it. This had happened in various degrees before, but never to this noticeable effect. The more love, care and consideration I poured into helping others with essential oils, the more I found clients flowed to me in expected and unexpected ways.

I stopped trying to control how my business was going to grow, how I was going to secure my fortune, and started to have fun.

The other thing I noticed when I joined doTERRA was how much fun I had with my 'team'. I had recognised how lonely it was sometimes as a therapist, it was just me, apart from the occasional people like virtual assistants I brought in to help me with specific tasks, or my time with coaches. The organisational structure of my business began and ended with me, and somctimes, in all honesty, that felt pretty overwhelming. I have always, always trodden my own path, but getting involved the doTERRA network marketing organisation enabled me to be part of something big which was powerful, ethical and for the greater good. It is a compassionate company, I have been convinced of that, and have yet to find anything to make me think otherwise.

That said, it is still up to every individual to make a decision and have their own standpoint as to how they feel, and their views on the products and organisation. This is where my occasional block came from.

I'll be honest here, sometimes I did want to run away and hide under a big rock, saying 'doTERRA? Me? No I've nothing to do with it'! These reactions mainly came from the strong views of the aromatherapy community, who were, and still are, launching a huge backlash against the company and its advocation of internalisation of their oils.

The same drum is being beaten time and time again, but again, as I have outlined before, when the surface is scratched they are value-based, subjective judgements, which are not rooted in any evidence, just personal and professional experiences.

To date, not one rant about doTERRA had advocated trying the oils and had negative reactions. The only bad press to have been spread far and wide, concerns individuals who had not followed safety information and had clearly been misinformed about how and when to use the oils, which is alarming.

That is why, as a therapist of 11 years, I believe I am in the best place to educate, support, and guide people who want to invest in these life-changing oils as well as train others in the uses of them to make sure the message is clear. Use them, but use them with care and consideration and in a way which takes responsibility for their potency and how powerful they are. We all have individual responsibility for our actions, and behaviour, and I see myself as a confidence-builder so people actually take the lid off and use their essential oils to their greatest benefit.

Wow, how far have I come?!

From a newly qualified therapist, ready and waiting for the world to open up and give me everything I wanted, to a therapist who has taken chances, embraced opportunities and learnt to trust her own judgement based on a constant evolution of understanding.

I am honest, I don't spend my weekends doing hours of CPD training designed to make me a 'better' or 'more qualified' therapist.

I have gone on a journey of personal development which has improved my confidence, and my ability to trust. It has empowered me to have faith in my decisions and deal with any wobbles. I have not done this alone. I have had the support of coaches, some of whom have been a complete mismatch, some who have let their own personal stuff take over their ability to support me, and some I have just grown beyond, not in a 'my business is too big' way. But their perceptions of who I am and what I can manage in my business are out of alignment with all the personal work I do on myself.

The essential oils have accelerated this

journey, exponentially, no kidding, and I cannot believe how much. Every single coach I have worked with, and everyone I will continue to work with have given me great lessons which I have learnt from.

For how do we know when we are successful if we haven't failed first? There is no one size fits all. No one can tell you 'how' to grow your business and grow in confidence as a therapist. But with the right nurturing and support, your business growth can certainly be accelerated beyond your expectations. Sometimes you will have to take action, and this might be scary, or feel too big, or too much to contemplate, but using the power of our subconscious, and the understanding of how our brain actually works to keep us stuck can make a transformational difference to how any business grows and thrives.

An underpinning of all of this, the true foundation of my continued success, is my family. I have been a therapist as long as I have been a mum, and this journey as a therapist with an emerging business has allowed me to access, and take care of my

children to the best of my ability.

This may be from an emotional point of view, using hypnotherapy or emotional healing, or, with homeopathy, and, most recently, essential oils. They are my why, my reason for doing what I do. When one of my children has an emotional outburst, I have learnt to look beyond the behaviour and understand why, and now I can administer oils along the way.

No one is perfect, but in building up my business I have, as a result, given myself space, and time, to be the mum I want to be. I don't spend my days exhausting myself with back- to-back clients. I spread my time, and energy so I can have balance between work and personal time, and that is my thrive, my success, not the amount of money in the bank or number of holidays or material possessions.

My husband doesn't always get what I do, but he has always been there when I do it. He provides those emotional foundations and understands my outpourings, and trusts that when I am going to do something, I do it, a bit like writing this book really!

So, there is no secret to success, no promise of riches. You can have all the money in the world, and still feel lost, and vulnerable, and lonely. If you let yourself be you, like I do, and continue to try to do (we are all works in progress) you will truly be able to avoid so many pitfalls as you grow your amazing therapy business, and enjoy doing it too.

Connect with the Author

I hope you've enjoyed this book and that it helps you realise that the opportunities to create a thriving therapy business could be right under your nose.

It would be great to keep in touch with you.

You can find me on social media:

www.facebook.com/ClareECogan

www.twitter.com/clarecogan

https://www.linkedin.com/in/clarecogan/

www.instagram.com/clarecogan

Or visit my website:

www.clarecogan.com

Printed in Great Britain
by Amazon